The New Organization

Colin Hastings

The New Organization

Growing the culture of
organizational networking

McGRAW-HILL BOOK COMPANY

London · New York · St Louis · San Francisco · Auckland
Bogotá · Caracas · Lisbon · Madrid · Mexico · Milan
Montreal · New Delhi · Panama · Paris · San Juan · São Paulo
Singapore · Sydney · Tokyo · Toronto

Published by
McGRAW-HILL Book Company Europe
Shoppenhangers Road, Maidenhead, Berkshire SL6 2QL, England
Tel: 01628 23432; Fax 01628 770224

British Library Cataloguing in Publication Data
Hastings, Colin.
 New Organization : Growing the Culture of
 Organizational Networking
 New ed.
 I. Title II. Series
 658.4

 ISBN 0-07-709284-8

Library of Congress Cataloging-in-Publication Data
Hastings, Colin.
 The new organization : growing the culture of organizational
 networking/Colin Hastings.
  p. cm.
 Includes bibliographical references and index.
 ISBN 0-07-709284-8
 1. Communication in organizations. 2. Organization. I. Title.
 II. Series.
 HD30.3.H375   1993
 302.2—dc20

McGraw-Hill

A Division of The McGraw·Hill Companies

12345 CUP 9876

Typeset by Datix International Limited, Bungay, Suffolk
and printed in Great Britain at the University Press, Cambridge.

Printed on permanent paper in compliance with ISO Standard 9706

To Nick, Matt and the other
three Wise Owls.

Contents

Contents

Part II   Growing the culture of organizational networking

Part III   The software of the New Organization

Acknowledgements

My work as an organizational consultant has brought me into contact with many companies and people who are searching for new ways of organizing and managing. Our joint quest has led me to meet and exchange ideas with a great number of people, all of whom helped mould the content of this book in some way or other. An important first milestone was a workshop in Barcelona in April 1989 at the European Forum for Management Development (EFMD) Research conference where Richard Mindel of BP, Cheryl Young of Inmarsat and I talked about the practical issues of developing networking organizations.

Another EFMD conference, this time in The Hague in June 1992, was the impetus for a further fruitful collaboration, this time with Lutz Reuter of Digital in Geneva, and Ada Demb, then at IMI in Lausanne and now Vice Provost for International Affairs at Ohio State University. Our preparation time together for a workshop on Networking Organizations laid the foundations of the Radar Screen model and many other insights. There are many more who have contributed, frequently I suspect without their even knowing. Kate Owen of BP extended my understanding of personal networking both by her ideas and by asking me to talk about it to BP managers. Course and workshop participants in BP Engineering (in particular Richard Manning and John Ellis), at DIEU in Copenhagen, at Neste in Helsinki, the Prudential Corporation in London, the World Health Organization in Belfast and Copenhagen and among ex-colleagues at Ashridge (in particular Kevin Barham and John Fripp)—all have provided invaluable inputs.

My three colleagues Wendy Briner, Julia Pokora and Frank Tyrrell who make up our consulting network, New Organisation Consulting, have continuously helped me to deepen my understanding of and to articulate more clearly the emerging dynamics of the New Organization that we all experience via our clients and between ourselves. Discussions with Bob Garratt about knowledge as an asset have been particularly thought provoking, as have those with Neil Spoonley. I am also most grateful to Tom Lester, a journalist working with *The Economist* Intelligence Unit and Business International. We both found ourselves writing about a similar topic, although with very different briefs.[1] Exchanging ideas and materials with him proved most beneficial.

Assembling information for each of the Pathfinder sections in the book required the help of a number of people. I heard Thomas Gasser, Deputy Chief

Executive Officer of ABB, talk brilliantly about his company. His head of corporate affairs Magne Roe has also been generous in commenting on drafts. John Fripp was able to add first-hand knowledge of Benetton. Elisabetta Prando of their Press Office was a fund of information. James Gallagher of Spatial gave me an agent's view of the DPE network and arranged for Martin Beale to comment on the draft. Michael Tobert gave me the supplier's side of the joint development project with the BP HSE Technology Team to develop BP's expertise database. Lutz Reuter in Geneva and David Skyrme and Keith Robinson in Reading, England, brought their already very deep understanding of this material to my description of Digital. Bram Breure, a director of Consultium in The Hague, had worked as a consultant for the KWS 2000 project in the Netherlands and was kind enough to send me a tape and give me a critique of my draft text. Huug van Dijkman of the Dutch Environmental Ministry also provided excellent and invaluable documentation, as well as helpful comments. Kristian Kreiner and Majken Schultz must take all the credit for their wonderful write up about the Danish biotechnology industry, which I simply summarized. Finally, some people I admire very much: Agis Tsouros, Ilona Kickbusch and Ron Draper of the World Health Organization Healthy Cities project taught me more than they can possibly realize about the soft networking aspects of the New Organization. Thank you, Pathfinders all.

Many other good people, of course, who I have never met have also played important parts in my thinking, consulting and writing. I hope very sincerely that all their names are mentioned in the references and acknowledgements throughout the book.

Finally, I come to the production and publishing process. Getting hold of relevant references has not always been easy and my thanks go to Andrew Ettinger and Beatrice Borer of the Ashridge Learning Resource Centre who were generous and prompt with their help. McGraw-Hill, through Julia Riddlesdell and Roger Horton, have proved to be a very professional, efficient and supportive team.

However, in a league apart is Isobel Exell, who has nursed this manuscript through many drafts and restructurings onto the word processor. Badly let down by software that proved not to be up to the task of a whole book, Isobel has kept going with a dogged persistence, a sense of humour and tremendous creative problem solving that I, and others, have treasured and admired. Her only peer can be Helen, my wife, herself a writer, who can bring that unique understanding of what it is like to produce a book and has provided wonderful loving and encouragement throughout. My special thanks, therefore, to these two wonderful women.

Colin Hastings
P.O. Box 2804
London
NW11 7LQ

Reference

1 Lester, Tom (1992) *The Managment Network Revolution Research Report M147*, Business International.

Introduction

It was Peter Drucker who suddenly crystallized the quest for me. I was reading his classic *Harvard Business Review* article, 'The Coming of The New Organization' shortly after its publication in early 1988.[1] He sketches a picture of what the large business organization of 20 years hence might look like. It was partly the symbolism of the title, the feeling it evoked that managers out there might be waiting for some organizational Messiah that stirred me. Beyond the realms of faith and hope, I realized that in my own consulting work and that of my colleagues that our clients, far from simply dreaming, were, in many small ways, getting on energetically with creating the New Organization, and they were doing it *now*.

The more I looked beyond my own direct experience, the more it became evident that there were organizations that seemed to be inventing the future. They were driven by some kind of vision of how they would need to operate if they were to survive and thrive in the twenty-first century. Gifford Pinchot[2] defines entrepreneurs as 'Dreamers who do' and that described them well.

I have selected a group of eight of these pioneering organizations and called them The Pathfinders. Some of them I have been privileged to work with and others I have learned about through other sources. Their stories form part of this book.

Part I describes the future directions that many organizations are trying to travel in. Many people use the term the networking organization or the networked organization as shorthand to describe this. I have found, however, that these terms cause much confusion. I refer instead to The New Organization.

Parts II and III concentrate on practical steps available to managers who want to get on with moulding these ideas to their own situations and making them a reality. I have used the concept of organizational networking as shorthand to describe the range of issues to be considered, capabilities to be developed and tools to be worked with in bringing the New Organization into being. The New Organization is the goal, the 'what'; organizational networking is the doing, the means, the 'how'.

The underlying framework of the book provides managers and students alike with a map for understanding both the what and the how more clearly. It does this by distilling lessons from my own consulting experience, from other writers and academics and from the early 'Dreamers who do', the Pathfinders.

It was Gareth Morgan[3] who first made us aware of the pictures or models we hold in our heads of organizations and how they work. His appealing models (see Figure I.1)[4] also represent, in more conventional terms, the common pictures that have characterized the (recent) history of the development of organizational forms. For it is only in the last 50 years or so that the traditional

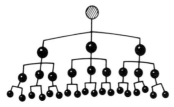

Model 1: The Rigid Bureaucracy

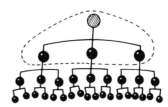

Model 2: The Bureaucracy with a senior 'management' team

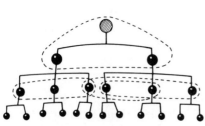

Model 3: The Bureaucracy with project teams and taskforces

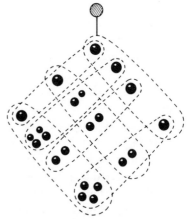

Model 4: The Matrix Organization

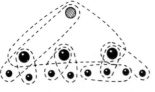

Model 5: The Project Organization

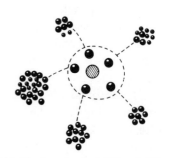

Model 6: The Loosely-coupled Organic Network

Figure I.1   A short history of organizational forms.

command and control model, derived from ancient military practice, has been seriously questioned.

The New Organization is the development and deeper understanding of Gareth Morgan's Models 5 and 6, the Project Organization and the Loosely-coupled Organic Network. The Pathfinder stories, the analytical frameworks and the suggestions for action given throughout the book all contribute to this. However, interspersed between the chapters you will find a totally different approach to understanding, an approach designed to stimulate your visual and imaginative faculties, to extend and enrich the images that help us to summarize and get a handle on the enormous complexity of concepts such as 'the organization' or 'managing'. Pictures convey through symbolism levels of meaning, complexity and subtlety that words and logical analysis cannot. One of the major barriers to people thinking in radically new ways about organization, lies in the paucity of images that managers use to represent 'the organization'. So, you will find between one chapter and the next different images described that just might provide you with new insights, language and metaphors of management and organizing. These imaginative interludes are called Pictures in the Mind.

References

1 Copyright © (1988) of the President and Fellows of Harvard College; all rights reserved. Reprinted by permission of *Harvard Business Review*. Peter Drucker (1988) 'The Coming of the New Organization,' *Harvard Business Review*, January–February, pp 45–53.
2 Pinchot, Gifford (1985) *Intrapreneuring*, Harper & Row, New York.
3 Morgan, Gareth (1986) *Images of Organizations*, Sage Publications, Beverley Hills, California.
4 Morgan, Gareth (1989) 'Bureaucracies to Networks: The Emergence of New Organizational Forms,' *Creative Organization Theory*, Sage Publications, Beverley Hills, California, p 66.

Part I
The quest for the New Organization

1
Breaking free—old models and new images

The greatest barrier to success will be outmoded views of what an 'organization' must look like and how it must be managed.

Raymond Miles, Dean, Business School, University of California and Charles Snow, Professor of Business Administration, Pennsylvania State University[1]

Our challenge in the next few decades will be to develop these new concepts and educational strategies, but I see some severe difficulties; these stem from the implicit assumption that organizations are fundamentally hierarchical. I hypothesize that we have great difficulty even imagining much less designing, nonhierarchical or even less hierarchical systems.

Ed Schein, Sloan School of Management, MIT[2]

The corporation as we know it is not dead, but it's ready for intensive care.

Mark Pastin and Jeffrey Harrison, Arizona State University[3]

1   Organizational Scrabble

The old rules

The way that we organize our enterprises and public bodies has remained essentially unchanged for several thousand years. Perhaps more importantly, the way we picture organizations in our minds and the way we think about how they work is deeply ingrained in every one of us. Which is why, when this traditional way of organizing begins to let us down, begins to show its inability to deal with quite momentous levels of change, we all find it difficult to see alternatives, let alone comprehend or implement them.

The symptoms of the traditional organization's inability to adapt are numerous. There are complaints from staff, workers and customers that decision making is very slow. Communication processes up and down the hierarchy are seen to be inefficient, with downward messages being distorted and upward messages failing to get through. Non-communication between departments, functions or specialisms is even more endemic, with the result that complicated problems needing

3

multifunction input are difficult to deal with. The culture thus created, the unwritten rules about 'how we do things round here', generally teaches people to keep their heads down and to limit their expectations. Such organizations are not breeding grounds for talent or initiative. The result is that they are slowly dying, killed by their slow response to rapidly changing environments, their lack of flexibility, their communications log jams and their failure to meet the changing expectations of their people and their customers.

All types of organization have struggled to overcome these problems with new products and services, by improving quality and customer care, by automating their production processes and by computerizing. However, a plethora of such change initiatives has had very mixed results. Gradually managers are realizing that none of these initiatives can solve the problems alone without changing the very organizational context within which they sit.

Organizational gridlock

Such organizations move all kinds of boundaries. These are visible and invisible barriers to the efficient passing on of hard information (facts, numbers, data) and soft information (expectations, judgements, feelings, opinions). The free flow of such communication is essential if an organization is to sense and interact in a healthy way with its changing environment. Such boundaries multiply (usually imperceptibly for those involved) until there comes the point of organizational gridlock.

Burgeoning boundaries

Boundaries between hierarchical levels, between departmental functions and professional specialisms have always been there, but they become more serious as organizations get bigger and specialisms proliferate. 'Bigness' means more locations in more countries. That means more impediments to communication both visible (physical distance) and invisible (the difficulties of understanding arising between different cultures). If different nationalities speak different languages, so do different professions, and even different specialisms within the same profession. The worlds of information technology, engineering, lawyers and personnel to name but a few, are full of 'colleagues' who cannot understand each other.

One should not underestimate the power of psychological boundaries. Most people on the shop floor, for example, would not dream of walking into the Managing Director's office for a chat about production issues. 'Oh, I can't do that' is an oft-heard phrase in traditional organizations. Lying behind this may be a lack of skill or confidence, some perceived personal risk in the course of action or clear rules that forbid it. Whatever the underlying reality, too many real or assumed boundaries begin to damage organizations that need to be responsive and flexible.

The prizes

The quest for the New Organization is forcefully driven by dissatisfaction with the old, but it is also driven by some new factors that create new possibilities. One of these is the potential of the new technologies that promise to revolutionize not only communications but also many of the basic assumptions behind the traditional models of organization. Another is the growing importance of so-called knowledge workers and a generally better educated workforce with higher levels of skill and different expectations. The third factor is the increasing globalization of markets and competition.

The prizes—the benefits of working out new ways of organizing—are, therefore, conceived of in terms of solving current organizational problems and grasping new opportunities. I hear managers searching for the prizes in asking such questions as:

- How do we learn to operate equally fluently at local, regional and global levels?
- How do we create successful partnerships with other organizations?
- How do we develop the abilities to respond rapidly and flexibly to changing circumstances?
- How do we attract and retain scarce talent?
- How can we continuously innovate, not only in products, but in business processes?
- How do we create the kind of organization where people will want to perform outstandingly?
- How do we get a grip on excessive property costs?
- How do we gain real added value from the new communications technologies?

No one should dismiss these managers because their questions are a little clichéd. The reasons managers should be taking New Organization ideas very seriously are stark and simple. Many of the organizations that they run are dinosaurs. They must fashion their organizations using the capabilities and tools they have at their disposal to do the complicated jobs that will be required of them in the twenty-first century. The old organization model is not up to the job. They will not survive unless they start to transform themselves. Such radical transformations will take decades—not months, as many managers believe.

Those organizations that start the soonest and learn how to develop these capabilities and tools most rapidly will have the competitive edge in the next century and will be the winners. Those who lag behind will not. It is as simple as that. What managers need, though, is some help in thinking through the alternatives and seeing what steps they can start to implement now.

The new rules

Try drawing a conventional organizational chart on a piece of paper. Place roles in boxes in the normal manner. Connect them together with vertical and horizontal lines in the traditional hierarchical organigram, putting the most senior people at the top and the more junior people at the bottom, and placing different functions across the page. Imagine that each of the boxes is a Scrabble piece and that these represent individuals, groups and locations. These Scrabble pieces become the elements of your New Organization.

Now enjoy yourself. Throw away the old rules. Rub out all the lines that connect the boxes together. The boxes are not now fixed on the page, but, like Scrabble pieces, can be moved around at will. Before you do that, though, rub out the squares on your *mental* Scrabble board. Jumble the pieces up. Add some further Scrabble pieces, perhaps of a different colour, to represent other organizations or people or groupings outside your organization who make a contribution in some way to its success. These might be contractors, suppliers, consultants or research institutions, for example. Put on each Scrabble piece some kind of hieroglyphic on it that describes its unique skills and experience.

You might choose to arrange these new pieces in a neat ring around your initial pieces. That is what most people do. Be more radical—mix them all up. Reassemble them in singles, pairs and small groupings and try clustering them in different combinations. Now try breaking free of another boundary—the flat surface. Arrange the pieces mentally in three-dimensional space. Imagine all the necessary lines of communication, the exchange of information and support between the different pieces and clusters that you believe would actually benefit your enterprise and help it to achieve its objectives more effectively. Imagine an open market operating between these different parties with none of the normal barriers to communication, such as turf protection, status, cultural differences or physical difficulties, getting in the way.

How do you react? Does this feel like a recipe for total chaos and anarchy? Or can you see in your mind some kind of an order within the apparent chaos. Is this a formless, structureless and ultimately unworkable image for you or is it an organism, teeming with life, energy and purpose? Examine your reactions honestly. Does it excite you or frighten you? In either case, read on, because this book has something for you. It also has something for your organization.

2   The hallmark of the New Organization

Having unscrabbled the traditional organization, leaving its elements—the people—scattered and in no fixed or clear relationship to one another, it quickly becomes apparent that in the New Organization it is the *nature* of these relationships between the elements that will be quite new. No longer can we rely on the false comfort of the neat and tidy relationships between functional and hierarchical roles displayed on the conventional organizational chart, because this has shown itself to be too rigid, too slow and insufficiently innovative. When we start instead seeing an organization as a constantly changing kaleidoscope of relationships between people, we begin to get a better flavour of what might be involved. To talk in IT jargon for a moment, people as the elements of organization and their structural relationships to one another constitute the *architecture* or the *hardware* of the New Organization. What I have called organizational networking, on the other hand, is the range of connective mechanisms and processes that need putting in place, both to hold all the elements together and to make it work—the *software* of the New Organization, if you like.

The type of organization that begins to emerge from these considerations has some very clear characteristics, as the Pathfinders' stories will reveal. I want to summarize these, however, at this early stage in order to help implant a slightly more concrete picture of the New Organization in your mind. I have called these characteristics the hallmark of the New Organization, summarized in Box 1.1.

Box 1.1   The hallmark of the new Organization

- Radical decentralization
- Intense interdependence
- Demanding expectations
- Transparent performance standards
- Distributed leadership
- Boundary busting
- Networking and reciprocity

Radical decentralization

The New Organization pursues a systematic and widespread approach to the decentralization of tasks, power and responsibility. This process, combined with a belief in 'small is beautiful' means that the organization is split up into many types of small, autonomous and accountable elements. The smallest element is the individual, who is provided with considerable autonomy but is also expected to exercise considerable accountability and responsibility.

Intense interdependence

The New Organization 'thinks' interdependence and multidisciplinary approaches. Many of its tasks are achieved by assembling coalitions and project teams to pursue common goals. Both individuals and the organization itself realize that in order to compete they have to cooperate.

Demanding expectations

The New Organization holds demanding expectations of itself. It sets strong, simple goals and has a clear sense of its purpose and mission. People throughout the organization demand that those who guide it ensure that this is provided. In addition, throughout the organization people are very demanding of each other. Each person has the right to ask for the cooperation of others.

Transparent performance standards

The New Organization sets demanding performance standards for everyone and measures and communicates these in a transparent fashion so that all are aware how they are doing in relation to other elements. The companies thus created are used to stimulate improvement not winners and losers.

Distributed leadership

The key relationships are built on the very wide exercising of responsibility among people, requiring of them considerable maturity and leadership qualities. These are people who are prepared to make things happen and who also share a sense of responsibility for the whole. Leadership moves beyond the boundaries of senior management into new networking roles.

Boundary busting

A systematic awareness and elimination of physical, personal, hierarchical, functional, cultural, psychological and practical boundaries and barriers to such cooperation and communication is a continuing process that is necessary to perpetuate the ability of the New Organization to stay flexible and adaptive.

Networking and reciprocity

Having shattered the rigid fabric of the conventional organization, the New Organization invests in the facilitation of intense communications between people. It thrives on direct relationships and information sharing between individuals in contact with each other, irrespective of considerations of role, status, level, functions, culture or location. Networking (which is explored in greater detail in the next chapter) is driven by a pervasive culture of reciprocity and exchange that mediates all relationships.

Box 1.2 Comparing cultures

Traditional cultures	New organization culture
• Adversarial relationships with 'outsiders'	• Searching for common goals with 'outsiders'
• Everyone in their place	• Everyone at the centre of their network
• Information available on a need-to-know basis	• Information available on want-to-know basis
• Dependence	• Independence
• Exclusivity	• Inclusivity
• Inward-looking	• Outward-looking
• Individuals given responsibility for parts only, not the whole	• Individuals assume responsibility for the whole
• Inhibition of talent	• Exhibition of talent
• Inaccessibility	• Accessibility
• Top down	• Inside out and outside in
• Boundary making	• Boundary breaking
• Under-communication	• Over-communication
• Independence	• Interdependence
• Compliance	• Empowerment
• External controls	• Self-regulation
• Asking for help is a weakness	• Asking for help is a strength
• Why do you want it?	• Yes of course, how can I help?
• Barriers to trade	• Free trade
• Insider dealing	• Fair dealing
• Hidden agendas	• Straight talking
• Span of control	• Span of communication
• Working against you to stop things happening	• Working with you to make things happen
• Passion for order	• Tolerance for ambiguity
• Mission statement	• A sense of mission
• Justifying communication	• Justifying confidentiality
• Interdisciplinary (relay approach)	• Multidisciplinary (Rugby approach)
• Technical specialists telling others	• Business-aware specialists learning from others
• Distaste for difference	• Delight in difference
• Power comes from retaining information (power over . . .)	• Power comes from sharing information (power to . . .)

3   Comparing cultures

Such characteristics create an organization with radically different structures and management processes to those of traditional organizations. They also create a climate or culture that operates through very different beliefs and values. Rather than try to explain these in great detail at this stage, it seems more useful to summarize them briefly in order to provide yet another snapshot of or perspective on the New Organization and to expand on these in the course of the rest of the book. Box 1.2 compares and contrasts the traditional organization culture with that of the New Organization. Part II of the book outlines five key areas (the roots of the New Organization) that need to be actioned by management in order that the New Organization culture can grow.

References

1 Copyright © 1986 of the Regents of the University of California. Reprinted by kind permission of the Regents. Raymond Miles and Charles Snow (1986) 'Network Organizations: new concepts for new forms', *California Management Review*, California Management Review XXVIII, 3.
2 Schein, Ed (1989) 'Reassessing the "Divine Rights" of Managers', *Sloan Management Review*, Winter.
3 Pastin, Mark and Jeffrey Harrison (1987) 'Social Responsibility in the Hollow Corporation', *Business and Society Review*, No. 63, Fall, pp 54–58.

Liquids

A friend reminded me of the concept of Brownian Motion we learned in elementary physics. If you look at the surface of your tea or coffee cup and observe the small particles of solids that are in suspension in the tea, you will see constant motion on the surface, a constant forming and re-forming of patterns as the different particles jostle with each other, interact with each other, move towards and away from each other. You will also notice that the particles cluster together into different shapes or groupings that change constantly. The same particle migrates frequently from being a part of one shape to being a part of another shape.

If you stir the liquid, you become aware of course that the particles and the currents that carry them are suspended in three dimensions, not just two on the surface. *Behind* the surface there is much more energy flowing between interacting particles than we can see just from the top. Nothing is still, nothing is fixed in relation to anything else, but it does stay fixed in the cup.

2
Making sense—understanding the different aspects of networking

We have to collaborate beyond borders and hierarchies. There must be no borders. We have to trade information, feedback, act as sensors for each other, exchange know-how, contact networks and skills . . .

Pauli Kulvik, Managing Director, Nest OY, Finland

1   Networking: what does it mean?

The theme of networking runs strongly through this book, like the blue veins in a good piece of Stilton or Dolcelatte. The word itself is a problematic one however as different people use it in different ways. Some use the phrase 'networking organization', but are unclear as to quite what it means. Others describe networking as a social process of linking and connecting individuals together, while others use it to talk about assembling coalitions or groups in order to achieve tasks. Just to complicate matters, the phrase the 'networked organization' is used in two ways: IT specialists use it when talking about the electronic exchange of information, while organization theorists use it when talking about ways in which different organizations become more interdependent on one another.

Such semantic confusion has compounded the difficulties of trying to create any coherent frameworks for understanding the New Organization. I have not been able to get away from the word, so will be using it in different ways (I hope somewhat more precisely) in building up such a coherent picture.

2   The radar screen model

In looking briefly thus far at the concept of the New Organization, we have challenged our thinking by looking at some of its key characteristics. We have also challenged the images that we hold in our heads and tried to sow the seeds of some different images that represent its networking nature more effectively. However, the human brain does find it easier if it can categorize. Management theorists in particular seem to be famous for inventing four-box models that purport to describe the world accurately. Inevitably, any categorization fails to

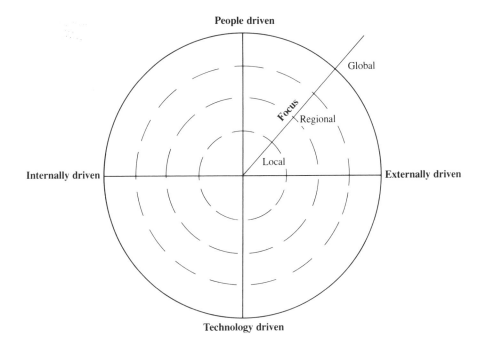

Figure 2.1 Dimensions of the new organization: the Radar Screen model. © Colin Hastings, New Organisation Consulting. (This diagram may be reproduced freely with due acknowledgement.)

capture *all* the complexities of the real situation, but it does help most of us clarify things somewhat.

The frameworks I shall be offering are not 'theory', they are patterns or ways of understanding that emerge from the early experiences of Pathfinders and others. Such innovators always travel through fog in the early stages of their journeys. Being modern organizations, I like to think that they have the benefit of radar and air traffic controllers to help them find their way. While all may *seem* like chaos and confusion at first, gradually some discernible and definable sense of pattern and order emerges as the radar's scanner rotates, repeatedly probing and revealing what lies ahead and around.

The radar screen itself provides a useful visual metaphor when describing the different dimensions of the New Organization. Figure 2.1 summarizes the four strategic logics that lead organizations to move towards one pattern or another.

Internally/externally driven

The horizontal axis describes whether the organization is primarily looking at the relationships between its internal elements (internally driven) or its relationships with external elements, other individuals and organizations (externally driven).

This internal–external axis is, of course, not an either/or, but what the axis *does* reflect is the organization's strategic rationale, starting point, emphasis or preference. It also says something about *what* the organization wants to be; its emerging sense of its identity as being relatively independent of other organizations or relatively interdependent with other organizations.

People/technology driven

The vertical axis describes its preferred ways of connecting these elements together. The top end is concerned with low-tech social processes (people driven) and the bottom with high-tech IT solutions (technology driven). Once again, these are not either/or dimensions, but questions of focus, starting point, preference and priorities. However, in expressing the primary means by which organizations choose to invest in creating internal or external connections and interlinking, they do also thereby express something of the organization's character and identity.

Local, regional or global focus

The rotating radar scanner itself (Focus in Figure 2.1) represents a geographical dimension of increasing distance between elements. These are described as local (within a country), regional (that is, Europe or the Americas or the Pacific Basin, say,) or global. These widening geographical viewpoints also reveal a psychological component of distance. This ranges from the relative comfort of the near and the familiar to the discomfort and unfamiliarity of the distant and the different. The further the geographical distance for communication, the greater it seems are the psychological, though not necessarily technical, barriers to communication and collaboration.

Organizational networking

Each strategic logic has, associated with it, a core networking process that has a clear purpose and is the primary means of implementing it. These are summarized in Box 2.1. I shall use the phrase *Organizational Networking* to refer to these four processes collectively.

I see organizational networking as the implementation of a range of social, cultural and technological processes that result in a devolution of power and responsibility and the breaking down of organizational boundaries. This facilitates direct person-to-person connections, sharing of information and joint working (both within and between organizations) in order to pursue common objectives, solve problems and satisfy the expectations of internal and external stakeholders more effectively and rapidly. Each of the four core networking processes are explained in greater detail in the following sections.

Box 2.1 Organizational networking

Strategic Logic	Core networking process	Purpose
Internally driven	Networking *within* the organization	Boundary busting
Externally driven	Networking *between* organizations	Successful partnerships
Technology driven	Hard networks	Connecting computers
People driven	Soft networking	Connecting people

3 Networking within the organization

Box 2.2 Gore—the Lattice Organization

The revolutionary fabric 'Goretex' is well-known to sports people. Bill Gore started the company that makes it, founding it on some startlingly original design principles, formulated when working as part of a highly productive and enjoyable taskforce at Du Pont. That was in 1958.

He dubbed his set of organizing principles 'the Lattice Organization'. First, there were no employees, only Associates. Every Associate dealt directly, person-to-person with every other, as they wanted and needed. Tasks were neither assigned nor assumed; Associates chose the areas in which they would like to contribute and then made personal, public commitments to themselves and others to make them happen. Discipline and feedback came from peers in the group involved in the implementation of tasks.

In addition, each Associate chose a 'Sponsor'. Sponsors were not bosses, but were asked to take a specific and personal interest in people, their contributions and their development. Sponsors and others acquired leadership by virtue of being asked to do so—what Gore called 'natural leadership', which is defined by followership.

Gore discovered by trial and error that Lattice principles work best in organization units of not more than 150 people. All Gore units therefore stay small. Each unit is composed of multiple overlapping lattices of people who work together or know each other. Liaison roles between lattices and between units play a crucial part.

Such a lattice is a paradox, said Gore, because it also needs strong direction and clear goals. These are initially provided by a founder or strong leader, but in time become heavily influenced by, and eventually emerge from the lattice itself. The sponsor system also serves to balance overall control and individual autonomy.

Gore suggested four guiding principles for all Associates to make the lattice work:

- *try to be fair* in all transactions inside and outside the enterprise
- *encourage growth and development* of skills, scope and responsibility in all fellow Associates
- *make commitments* and stick to them
- *consult* with others before taking any action that might threaten the business.[1,2]

Networks

The purpose of networking within organizations is to break down boundaries and create quick and open person-to-person communications. While stimulating networking is a general strategy that sets a style and culture for an organization, the creation of *specific* networks or groupings of individuals that cut across the various parts of the organization can also serve to focus activity, know-how and people with similar interests. For example, BP's corporate centre and business have highlighted particular opportunity areas for the creation of networks and have also defined what the roles and purposes of such boundary-spanning networking might be (see Figure 2.2[3]). Other companies are building networks around important business processes such as quality, customer service and new product development.

Such internal networks are branded in some way, usually by the topic of interest that network members share. Examples might include application areas for a new technological process, gathering and sharing information on the Russian market or approaches to minimizing ground water pollution. In some companies, such as Digital, networks exist for leisure and social pursuits as well. Networks exist for a purpose, to achieve something both for the organization and those participating. Networking—the open asking for and sharing of ideas, experience and information—is how they do it. Many networks of this nature can be most easily 'seen' in the form of ongoing computer conferences within the organization or through network newsletters, meetings and conferences.

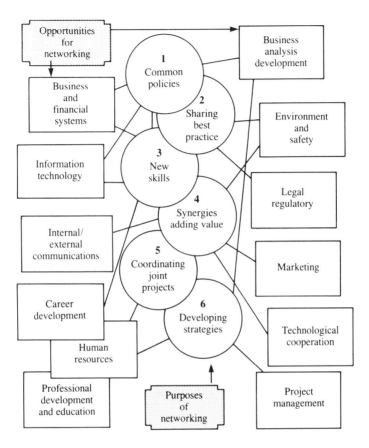

Figure 2.2   The opportunities for and purposes of networking in BP.

The delusion of delayering

The purpose of boundary busting is to create organizations that can respond rapidly and flexibly, free of the constraints of traditional hierarchical and functional rules of communication. There is much talk among managers and popular theorists in this context of the flat, flexible organization. It is unfortunate that this concept has led many to believe that they can achieve the prizes of the New Organization simply by cutting out layers of the hierarchy, so-called delayering.

Such people talk about flattening the *hierarchy* but not about flattening *lateral barriers* to communication and team working. Recently flattened hierarchies end up being flatter, yes, but even more inflexible because some of the roles responsible for lateral communication, inefficient as they may have been, have been cut out. It is not surprising, therefore, that senior managers frequently complain that their flattened organizations are experiencing team-working problems. Of course they are—the people left have never had to take any responsibility for communicating or collaborating with other disciplines or functions, let alone talking directly with senior management. They have been told in the past to stay rigidly within their own defined areas and be specialists. Delayering alone, therefore, is not sufficient to create the networking and communication processes across the organization that are the engines of flexibility.

We need the innovative metaphor of the New Organization to replace the flat, flexible myth. Flatter hierarchies are here to stay, but so too are the flattened walls between departments and specialisms. Networking processes built up in many ways over a long period of time will provide the desired openness and elasticity of structure and communication processes.

Federal Express' networked organization, for example, links together its offices throughout the world in a sophisticated electronic information sharing system designed to create competitive advantage in the international parcels distribution business. Its main application of this communications technology at first was just within its own organization, but over time it has gradually come to be used by its customers, too. The technology is used both to break down barriers and, simultaneously, bind together the different parts of its global, far-flung empire, creating instant communications independent of time and space.

The much-publicized networking aspirations of BP[4] are, again, primarily internally driven. Its objective is to maximize the communication, speed of decision making and synergy between the different parts of BP. In this case, the more social technology of culture change has been the preferred method of implementation.

4   Networking between organizations

Box 2.3   AMEC

AMEC, one of the UK's leading construction and engineering enterprises, has been systematically building its strength in the chemicals sector. The key to AMEC's overseas thrust, however, is the 20 per cent stake it took in French engineering specialist Serete which gives AMEC an important holding in the independent group, and a presence in France, Italy, Spain, Portugal and Germany. These add to its existing continental operations in the Netherlands (Matthew Hall Keynes) and Portugal (a 50 per cent stake in Engil), and those in the US through its 50 per cent holding in construction management company Morse-Diesel. . . . AMEC hopes eventually to be able to offer multinational companies a single source of contracting expertise, no matter which country the project is in. . . . The Serete move, in particular, enhances AMEC's position in Europe. The partnership has already led to substantial benefits, citing projects for which the companies have put in a joint bid, whereas individually a bid would not have been possible.

Another innovation that Ferguson believes will eventually give AMEC a head start over its established rivals is its commitment to the concept of 'partnership'. Instead of each project proposal going out to tender to a number of contractors, the aim is to establish a long-term agreement between AMEC and the customer so that a series of projects can be handled over time. The benefits, explains Ferguson, are that the two companies learn to trust each other and work closely together. . . . 'What's the point of taking a lot of time learning how to work with one customer when as soon as the next project comes up it can go to any number of contractors and the learning process has to start all over again?' asks Ferguson. 'This cannot be the route to quality' . . . Ferguson believes the strategies being pursued by AMEC in the chemicals field could make it a major player by the end of the decade.

European Chemical News, 7 October, 1991

The pressures to cooperate

As the sophistication of technology grows in areas such as health, pharmaceuticals, aircraft, space and defence equipment, the cost of developing new technologies has escalated in an exponential fashion. So great has been this rise that even the largest companies cannot afford to take the risks of investing alone in research and development. The quest for quality as well as the costs and complexity of servicing increasingly global markets is forcing organizations into collaborating with their clients, their suppliers and frequently their competitors in many new ways. As a result, many new patterns of partnership are being created.

Patterns of partnership

Such pressures are forcing even the largest and richest of organizations into different forms of cooperation. The rush of joint ventures and strategic alliances in the early to mid 1980s (which shows no signs of abating) was testament to these developments. Diane Wilson, a researcher and faculty member in the Sloan School of Management at the Massachusetts Institute of Technology, in surveying the research on strategic alliances says,

inter-firm ventures have long been an important element in the investment of US and foreign manufacturing firms, but in recent years not only has the number of strategic alliances between US, Japanese and European enterprises increased dramatically . . . but the nature of these ventures has changed, representing what may be a shift in traditional patterns of new product development . . . such inter-firm relationships are not arms length, but involve the shared control of technological, production and marketing assets and significant contributions of managerial and technological expertise by all the partners involved in the alliance.[5]

Another variation on the strategic alliance is the 'dynamic network'. Amstrad, the electronics group, for example, is closely linked and interconnected with a range of suppliers throughout the world. Amstrad is not vertically integrated, which means that it does not have all the different stages in the production and marketing process under its own name and control. Raymond Miles,[6] at the University of California, who coined the phrase dynamic network, describes it as a form of collaboration between different organizations, each with their own unique strengths, some in marketing, some in distribution, some in production, some in R&D, with one company. In this case, Amstrad acts as the 'broker' orchestrating their diverse contributions. Increasingly, the big names in the international fashion industry, for example, operate in this way.

Such strategic alliances or dynamic networks are not, however, confined to large multinationals. They now provide mechanisms for small and medium-sized enterprises to operate globally. Cooperative networks of local service organizations whose clients' operations spread across borders are increasingly common among smaller legal firms, advertising agencies, consultancies, arts organizations and business schools. Equally, between government agencies, particularly in such areas as international crime and drug trafficking, there are extensive links. Interpol has been working successfully since long before the phrase strategic alliance was coined. Similarly, interagency networks in the fields of disaster relief and Third World development are rapidly learning how to manage themselves effectively. A common theme in these partnerships is the virtue of obtaining the benefits of scale efficiency and market visibility while *also* being able to respond to local requirements.

Such collaborations are based on the principle that the independence and autonomy of groups and other organizations is both recognized and valued. Simultaneously, however, there is the requirement that these autonomous elements become much more actively interconnected and interlinked. A primary condition that needs to be met if this interconnecting is to be effective is not only that there should be the infrastructure in place for making connections, but that fast, open, accurate exchange of information—both inside and outside organizations—should be possible. The new culture of partnership also needs to be developed.

There is also a growing plethora of partnership relationships between large and small organizations. Large ones gain access to and support the development of innovative ideas by taking shareholdings in business startups. Others develop informal links. One such instance among many was in the downsizing within IBM in the UK. Keen to let go, but not to lose precious skills and talent, they encouraged an idea put forward by two departing Human Resource professionals that they could act as brokers who would record, search out and sell back to IBM relevant skills from among the network of those who had been 'let go'. In this manner, Skillbase was born—a form of agency, hiring to IBM, ex-IBM people. On this foundation has been built a successful business that services not only IBM, but also its network of skilled professionals and many new clients keen to have access to this experienced resource.

Strategic mentality

The internally driven and externally driven strategic logics, and their associated local, regional or global focus, require very different kinds of mentality. The internally driven mentality is about having a wide range of your own resources and seeking to maximize their use within and across the organization by means of high-quality communications and the breaking down of internal boundaries. The externally driven mentality is about recognizing what resources your organization does not have; it is about partnership with other organizations that can provide you with what you need.

Given some of the inexorable trends in world business and economics at the moment, many organizations will have to go beyond the internal/local dimension towards the external/global. Even those staying local are going beyond decentralization and outsourcing many of their requirements. Many underestimate the shift in mentality that is required to go from the one to the other, from having control of *all* your resources to having *shared* control. Having small, local, external, focused networks on the peripheries may be relatively comfortable, but the acid test, the acid difference, is when the fundamental structure of the organization becomes externally focused towards partnership and when it goes beyond the local market. It is inevitable that organizations will have to operate right along this spectrum in the future and will have to become good both at internal networking processes and the creation of external (local, regional and global) networks of cooperating organizations.

It is this mentality of partnership that will characterize externally driven organizations. It is, for many, a new skill that has to be learned, especially in organizations that have historically had at best arm's length, if not outright adversarial relationships with suppliers, competitors, customers or their own counterparts in other countries.

5   Hard networks—connecting computers

Box 2.4   Transformation through IT

A large international accountancy firm developed the following statement of intent on future IT strategy.

Effective networking is essential to achieve our business objectives and to make the New Organization work.

Information systems and technology will support networking in a number of ways, giving rise to four different perspectives.

1 The clients' perspective

(a) Clients will be able to identify the right people with the right skills by using the on-line expertise database.

(b) Clients will be able to communicate electronically with our staff by means of electronic mail and join electronic conferences on a world-wide basis.

(c) Clients will be able to order services and, where appropriate, monitor progress electronically. Deliverables and invoices will also be transmitted electronically.

(d) The system will allow project teams to interwork remotely, utilizing both our own and client staff. A client overview will also be provided.

(e) On-line access to technical databases will be provided.

2 Our professional's perspective

(a) Access to on-line expertise database, E-mail and electronic conferencing will be provided to every 'home-team' professional and 'away-team' professionals where feasible. This will facilitate intra-organizational communications regardless of location or time zone.

(b) Technical information will be held in databases accessible through the network in as transparent fashion as possible.

(c) When working in project teams, the system will facilitate effective interworking and simultaneous access.

(d) Groups of professionals in the same function will be able to share data by extending their desktop storage into shareable 'central' storage in a transparent fashion.

(e) An electronic 'bulletin board' will be available to all staff to encourage information sharing and help maintain our sense of identity.

(f) Electronic links to the system's infrastructure will be provided to those members of staff who need to work from home.

3 The management's perspective

(a) Senior managers will have direct access to all staff-related data needed to carry out their staff management functions, including resource utilization, career development, training and salary reviews.

(b) Managers will be able to access financial and other key performance data on-line and on demand.

4 The supplier's perspective

Quotations, orders and payments will be made by electronic data interchange (EDI). In addition, major suppliers and contractors will be given access to our communications infrastructure, subject to making the appropriate security arrangements.

The potential of information and communications technology is truly the stuff that dreams are made of. You can see the gleam in the eye when people in the field start talking about what can now be done. 'Availability of information anywhere and at any time for anybody' is the kind of slogan behind the passion.

Information

We used to send letters through the post. Now we send 'letters' through the electronic mail system. But E-mail, though the most familiar technology to many is but the tip of the electronic iceberg. Equally we can send a picture or a diagram. Using videoconferencing, people can talk to and see each other live at opposite sides of the world. The technology can compress an audio tape and send its contents electronically. The same can be done with video material, as we see dramatically illustrated daily on our television screens with live reports from all around the world.

Using these technologies, individuals can potentially communicate very rapidly. They can not only send, but also ask for things and obtain replies within hours, if not minutes. The information they are swapping is a much broader commodity than many people realize. Think of it instead as the immediate delivery of products and services anywhere at anytime for anybody. That is the potential that lies, tantalizingly, at our fingertips.

Communications technology

Imagine a company that has locations all over the world. Put PCs on the desks of all employees in all those locations and connect them together. Some of these connections, say within a building, will be made by cables or even nowadays using microwaves instead. Buildings within the same country may be connected together using that country's telephone system and optical fibres. Countries are connected together most frequently by satellites that scoop up information from one sending station on the ground, transmit it down to a receiving station in another country, which in turn pipes that information through the country's optical fibre system to its ultimate destination, all in a matter of microseconds. This is what I shall be calling the hard network, the 'architecture' of modern communications systems.

The original applications of IT were about connecting computers together and having them 'talking' to each other to replace or automate the human component. Such EDI (Electronic Data Interchange) is still big business. Certainly, the world's financial markets could not now work without it. Neither could many large store chains who automatically track sales, stock levels and product delivery schedules in this manner.

More recently, however, the focus has begun to be on communications and, in particular, on enhancing communication between people. E-mail, fax, digital telephone services, videoconferencing and much else besides, hugely expands the potential for interactions and interdependence.

Connectability

The technology is hugely complex. Box 2.5 gives a sense of this complexity as well as a useful guide to the area. The components of IT are hugely expensive and bedevilled by a lack of agreed international standards.

Box 2.5   The vocabulary of computer networks

Band width The capacity of the network to carry information.

Bits per second (BPS) A measure of how much information a network can carry.

Bridge A computer device that allows networking between different computer systems.

Cable A wire that carries the networking signals between computers. Many different cable designs are used and most networks must be configured to use the particular cable design that is available.

Gateway A computer device that allows two different networks to function more or less as if they were one.

Interface card The device that plugs into the computer and allows it to communicate over a network. Each network and cable combination requires a particular interface card.

Interoperability The condition when two computers can function very reliably and intricately together over a network.

Local area network (LAN) A network confined to a relatively small area and generally containing a relatively small number of computers. No hard definition exists.

Metropolitan area network (MAN) A network confined to a single city or town, often (but not necessarily) containing more computers than a LAN.

Network A system by which two or more computers can send and receive files of information, access each other's disks and other resources and otherwise communicate.

Network computing A term intended to replace LANs, MANs and WANs, reflecting that these distinctions now make very little sense from a technological or a user standpoint.

Network management The process of monitoring and controlling the size, configuration, speed, efficiency, utilization and other features of a network.

Node A device connected to a computer network. It is most often a computer, but under some network designs it may be a printer, scanner, disk storage device, terminal or other device.

Operating system The internal codes a computer uses to perform basic functions, including file storage and retrieval, information display and capture and the operation of an application program.

Protocol A procedure by which computers exchange information and verify the accuracy of the information exchanged. Networking protocols are highly specific and complicated and are subject to the control of international bodies.

Router A computer device that determines which of two or more wires should receive a signal originated by another computer.

Server A computer device that supports other devices on a network. File or disk servers store and retrieve files for other computers. Network servers manage the networking signals passed between other computers on a network and may also provide file services.

Sneaker set The practice of carrying computer disks from one computer to another to exchange information by people wearing sneakers.

Topology The physical design of the network, including the actual wiring in use and the arrangement of computers along that wire.

Wide area network (WAN) A network that is not confined to any geographical area. WANs now circle the planet and include satellite links in place of long-distance cables. Many WANs contain tens of thousands of separate computers, from super-computers to PCs, as well as dozens or hundreds of MANs and LANs. The most elaborate WANs are indistinguishable from LANs to the user.

Journal of Accountancy,
December, 1990.

In order to realize the full potential of the technology within an organization, the pressures build up for what John Spackman[7] has called the integrated corporate information network. Realizing this concept is so complicated, so challenging and so political that there are few organizations that can honestly claim to have achieved it.

If it is a complicated enough process to project manage the implementation on an integrated corporate network within the same organization, imagine the next level of complexity when you are trying to connect together the IT systems of quite separate organizations. The problems of connectability are immense, but it is being done successfully. GFT the Italian designer label[8] and JC Penney the giant US Retailer,[9] in parallel with significant parts of the international fashion industry, connect together many of their different producers, suppliers and customers in huge global networks. Motor manufacturers, such as General Motors and Nissan, connect together their production plants, their suppliers and, increasingly, their dealers. This is not only a prerequisite for 'just-in-time' delivery of components, it is part of a wider customer service strategy that envisages customers sitting in the dealer's showroom choosing on the computer (from many options) their detailed specification, with guaranteed delivery just days later.

Strategy

A commitment to hard, high-tech networks involves major strategic decisions and huge capital investment in a field where the technology is changing rapidly. The IT world is gradually learning how to make this technology more flexible and adaptable, but, even so, any decision in this area lays a company open to major uncertainties and risks associated with investment in the architecture of the system. Such strategic decisions and the subsequent problems of effective implementation consume large amounts of management time in an area where many of them feel both impelled to act, but, simultaneously, ignorant and fearful.

There are still many managers who hope to bypass IT, but they cannot—its potential is too huge. It is only when managers start to become informed and demanding clients for IT specialists, rather than abdicating responsibility to the technologists, that progress will be made in getting what is needed out of the technology rather than simply accepting (and frequently rejecting) what the technology offers. Equally, the myth that installing electronic communications will of itself 'create' the New Organization and organizational networking has to be challenged. IT is not the answer to corporate transformation; it is only a part of the wider organizational networking solution.

6   Soft networking—connecting people

Box 2.6   Yorkshire Health Associates

> Reform of the UK's National Health Service in the late 1980s required many people in the medical profession to take on greater managerial roles. Helen Jones' role was to enable this development process for doctors. 'We were asking doctors to move from an established and known territory onto uncertain and shifting terrain. . . .'

She observed that doctors had no connections with the manage-ment area that would enable them to work on developing their managerial skills. So, she set out to build bridges between the medical and managerial worlds. She brought an initial group of several different independent management development consultants in to a network and it designed programmes with the doctors to meet their needs.

In turn, Helen identified several target groups within the medical establishment. Within each of these—newly appointed Consultants, Pathologists, General Practitioners and Practice Managers, for example—she had found one or more key individuals who were enthusiastic and keen to learn and develop. They networked and sold the idea to their colleagues while Helen fed in new management development consultants who could meet their learning needs.

Different external consultants were now also working simultane-ously with more than one medical group, making linkages between problems and ideas and putting people in different disciplines, who had previously had little contact with each other, in touch to discuss their common managerial problems. Helen was also pulling in the medical educational establishment, which previously had not seen managerial education as being included in its remit, gradually reshaping their view of their role. Beyond her network of consult-ants, Helen also linked a number of her medical colleagues into an innovatory programme at Ashridge, the international business school based in the UK, in which doctors and managers from industry were brought together on a series of development pro-grammes. Not only did this enable her doctors to extend their external networks to industrial and service managers (each of whom had much to learn from the other) but to other doctors in other regions going through similar problems.

Helen runs regular conferences that bring together all the external consultants with their medical clients. They work together on how to improve the effectiveness of the overall learning network. Through such soft communications mechanisms and by branding the whole as Yorkshire Health Associates, she has also made what might have otherwise been an invisible process visible to all. In so doing, she has unleashed a self-sustaining drive for management development among the Yorkshire medical profession.[10]

By soft networking I mean all the different ways in which people make, and are helped to make, connections with each other. Through the systematic use of a wide range of soft technologies, such as conferencing, mobility policies and travel, for example, organizations accelerate the weaving of complicated patterns of communication, understanding and learning inside and outside their formal boundaries.

Many managers may think that their huge investments in hard technology suggest that the soft technologies are no longer so important, particularly in times of cost reduction. This is a fundamental mistake. The whole thrust of this book suggests that the soft technologies need to come *first*, to form the infrastructure of personal contacts throughout and between organizations. The hard communications technologies *follow* to support and enable those personal connections to expand and flourish. However, in order to do this, soft networking, most often just taken for granted, needs to be better understood, more carefully and systematically nurtured and more heavily invested in.

The informal organization

In the context of work organizations, however, networking often has a negative connotation. It is often associated with 'the old boy network' or being 'political'. Any society will provide stories of how difficult it is to break into their closed, exclusive club. Fraternities in the USA, the Oxbridge factor in the UK and the Grandes Ecoles in France are but a few examples of these closed networks. It is not surprising, therefore, that many feel cynical about the process that they see as meeting the needs of the very few. It is not surprising that they experience many boundaries that are difficult to communicate across.

It is ironic therefore, to find that in many conventionally structured organizations, soft networking is indeed taking place at *all* levels in the organization and cutting across both functional and hierarchical boundaries. This is what organization theorists and sociologists have come to call 'the informal organization'. Those with courage and the need to get things done quickly frequently break the rules in the interests of unblocking the log jam of communication that happens when you do follow the rules. Wise managers realize that it has only been this unofficial organization that has been prolonging the life of dinosaurs. It is the rediscovery of and investment in the informal organization that is unleashing potential as significant, if not more so, as that provided by the new hard technologies.

The power of soft networking has also been highlighted by other experiences. The peace movement and the anti-Vietnam movement in the USA demonstrated how successful an informal but orchestrated network of individuals and groups could be. The women's movement has shown how large-scale influence can be exerted through the work of relatively small numbers of dedicated individuals with a common cause. A quite different and rather more chilling example of network power and resilience is the way in which terrorist groups operate.

Connections: letting go of hangups

Rosabeth Moss Kanter, Professor of Organization Management at Yale University, in her seminal study *The Change Masters*,[11] showed how change agents or product champions within innovative organizations systematically cultivated and mobilized networks of people to help them bring about innovations and change. These were not people being 'political', using connections for private goals, they were people being effective. Soft networking was an important part of building individuals' confidence and sense of positive power. She defined positive power as the ability to make things happen. This positive power was exercised, not in the narrow self-interested ways that characterize the political approach to networking (which she called negative power—the power to stop things happening), but to serve the overall strategic goals and purpose of the organization. All this was achieved by building connections or networks.

Currencies

Professor Moss Kanter's research demonstrated very clearly how the process of making connections created a trade in different resources and 'currencies' of great importance to individuals in getting things done. By means of skilful networking, individuals built the credibility, skills and the clout to mobilize the key resources of money, materials, time and people. Likewise, networking provided them with access to important soft information—being in the know, having early warnings about important decisions that were going to be made that might affect their projects, access to information of a technical nature or access to people's expertise either inside or outside the organization and so on. The connections also provided the important currencies of support and cooperation from key people within the organization. These change masters were indeed skilful in obtaining backing for what they felt needed doing, gaining approval and legitimacy and being able to make a good case. Much of this came from their ability to develop quality relationships through networking within the organization.

External networks

Another interesting strand of research comes from a study of entrepreneurs and the innovation process in small companies. Roy Rothwell[12] at the Science Policy Research Unit at Sussex University, England, highlighted the vital role that external linkages to sources of technical and market expertise played in successfully innovating small companies.

Carlos Jarillo, Professor of Strategic Management at IMD, the international business school in Lausanne, Switzerland, has also studied the importance of external networks to entrepreneurs. In surveying the academic literature in this area he comments,[13] it is an essential characteristic of entrepreneurs to end up using more resources than they control for they are motivated primarily by the pursuit of opportunity, rather than feeling constrained by using the resources they control . . . Networking is, in most instances, the method entrepreneurs use to get access to external resources. . . . Thus, the realization of the importance of (external) networking and the understanding of the skills involved in making it succeed are two of the most important 'entrepreneurial skills' that can be taught and developed.

Reciprocity

Soft networking gets things done without the formal exercising of traditional sources of power and authority. It works on different levels to those of command and control that are the tools of the traditional hierarchy.

Understanding the concept of reciprocity is important to understanding *how* the process of networking gets things done. Reciprocity lies at the heart of cooperative behaviour, which is the New Organization's primary means for making things happen. David Bradford and Allan Cohen have researched the idea of reciprocity. Their ideas have been well summarized by Kevin Barham[14] of Ashridge Management Research Group.

According to David Bradford and Allan Cohen . . . the fundamental way to acquire influence without formal authority is through the 'law of reciprocity'—'the almost universal belief that people should be paid back for what they do; the one good (bad) deed deserves another'. They suggest that people should use the metaphor of 'currencies' and 'exchange rates'. In addition to organizational technical knowledge, possible currencies that people can trade include 'inspiration-related' currencies such as vision—being involved in a task that has larger significance for the unit, companies, customers or society; or a 'position-related' currency such as involvement in a task that can aid promotion or advancement; or a 'relationship-related' currency such as giving personal support.

Managers must think about the other person as a potential ally, not an adversary. They need to know the other person's world, including their needs and goals. They need to be aware of the key goals and available resources that the other person may value. And they must seek mutual gain rather than 'winner takes all'.

The greater extent to which the manager has worked with the potential ally and created trust, the easier the exchange process will be. Each knows the other's desired currencies and pressures and each will have developed a mutually productive style for interacting. Less time is spent on figuring out the intentions of the ally, and there is less suspicion about when the payback will occur. Two things matter: success in achieving task goals and success in proving the relationship so that the next interaction will be even more effective. Too often, say Bradford and Cohen, people who want to be effective concentrate on the task and act as if there is no tomorrow. It might be added that reciprocity will be even more effective when it is based on friendship, as in the female approach to networking. . . . Research suggests that women's behaviour patterns emphasize precisely those values and attitudes that are important for networking, such as sensitivity, communication, community, sharing and relationships. Women are also able to shift interactions from power and dominance modes to cooperative modes. They tend to be more concerned with the social dimension of work and more inclined to view work relationships as friendships. They are also more concerned than men to listen and to pay attention to others' points of view. Whilst this is a natural skill for many women, it is a skill that men only learn as they get older.

Carlos Jarillo and Howard Stevenson echo these findings in their study of the growth of partnerships and other cooperative (rather than competitive) strategies between businesses and organizations.[15]

Here we see the main characteristic of a successful cooperative arrangement; the long-term outlook of the participants. If it is absent, we fall immediately into the competitive zero sum game . . . If the players take a long-term outlook where what matters is the maximization of profits over many deals, each specific instance loses criticality; what matters is not to make the most money now, but to keep the relationship going. In fact, maintaining the relationship becomes a valuable end in itself, which greatly facilitates agreement. A hard-nosed business-man, a profit maximizer, will cooperate. . . .

Companies that have been able to set up powerful cooperative arrangements go out of their way to foster trust. They not only take a long-term, joint-maximization view of the relationships, but make sure that they are seen to do so. In many cases, as in Benetton, personal contacts help immensely. In others, it must be based on a history of trust-inducing behaviour. Trust is hard to create and can be broken in a second. But not being able to elicit trust is extremely expensive: few companies can compete against the whole world.

There is certainly an increasingly strong body of research demonstrating the superior results that flow from reciprocity and cooperation.[16,17] As Carlos Jarillo and Howard Stevenson conclude, 'the evidence in favour of cooperation is, by now, too strong to ignore'.[18] Managers had better start learning how to do it!

References

1 Gore, W L (1985) 'The Lattice Organization: a philosophy of enterprise', *Networking Journal*, Spring/Summer 1, pp 24–28.
2 Rhodes, Lucien (1982) 'The Un-manager', *INC*, August, pp 35–43.
3 By kind permission of Roy Williams, Director of Development and Learning, BP, March, 1990.
4 Butler, Steven (1990) 'Cutting Down and Reshaping the Core', *Financial Times*, 20 March.
5 Wilson, Diane (1989) 'A Process Model of Strategic Alliance Formation in Firms in the Information Technology Industry', Paper 90s:89-070. Sloan School of Manage-ment, Massachussetts Institute of Technology.

6 Miles, Raymond and Charles Snow (1986) 'Network Organizations: new concepts for new forms', *California Management Review* XXVIII, 3.
7 Copyright © 1988. Reprinted by permission of John Wiley & Sons Ltd. Spackman, John (1991), ETIS, Brussels, Belgium, personal letter.
8 Howard, Robert (1991) 'The Designer Organization: Italy's GFT goes global,' *Harvard Business Review*, September–October.
9 Kamman, Alan, *Global Networks, Stage by Stage*, Nolan Norton & Co, Lexington, Massachusetts.
10 Jones, Helen (1992) Yorkshire Health Associates, mimeo.
11 Moss Kanter, Rosabeth (1983) *The Change Masters*, George Allen & Unwin, London.
12 Rothwell, Roy (1991) 'External Networking and Innovation in Small and Medium-Sized Manufacturing Firms in Europe', *Technovation*, Vol. II, No. 2, Elsevier, pp 93–111.
13 Jarillo, Carlos (1988) 'On Strategic Networks', *Strategic Management Journal*, Vol. 9, pp 31–41.
14 Barham, Kevin (1991) 'Networking—the corporate way round international discord', *Multinational Business*, No. 4, pp 1–11.
15 Copyright © 1991. Reprinted by permission of Pergamon Press Ltd. Carlos Jarillo and Howard Stevenson (1991) 'Cooperative Strategies—the payoffs and the pitfalls', *Long Range Planning*, Vol. 24, No. 1, pp 64–70.
16 Axelrod, Robert (1984) *The Evolution of Cooperation*, Penguin Books, London.
17 Crawford, Lynn (1992) 'Negotiate or Litigate: conflict management in the project process'. A presentation at the International Project Management Conference in Florence measured dramatic differences in construction project performance when cooperative strategies as opposed to confrontational strategies were used in the relations between clients, architects, contractors and subcontractors. University of Technology, Sydney, Australia.
18 Jarillo, Carlos and Howard Stevenson (1991) (see ref. 15).

Molecular structures

Another scientific image helps us to break away from the two-dimensional limitations of writing or drawing things on bits of paper.

Imagine one of those models of molecules that one sees in textbooks or, perhaps, in television programmes, where individual atoms are represented by differently coloured balls of different sizes, interconnected by a fine web or lattice of sticks. There is a fascinating children's construction set that uses a similar process, connecting highly coloured plastic pieces with bendy tubes.

This kind of three-dimensional molecular image gives us a sense of interconnections. Perhaps these interconnections are a little bit too rigid, but if one thought of simulating the same kind of three-dimensional model on a computer, it would be very easy to change the kinds of interconnections between people constantly. It would be easy to simulate the flows of both hard and soft information between different individuals and groups of individuals.

I like this image, too, because the molecular model can be turned upside down, it can be twisted, pulled . . . there is no inherent sense of hierarchy, of people being at the top or at the bottom.

3
Three Pathfinders—a range of different approaches

And thus do we of wisdom and of reach[a]
With windlasses[b] and with assays of bias,[c]
By indirections find directions out.
William Shakespeare, *Hamlet*

a = Practical ability
b = Roundabout approaches
c = Improvisation

1   Scanning for Pathfinders

To me, the word Pathfinder signifies people who are trail blazing, people who are innovators setting off on a journey towards a dream without knowing in detail how they will get there nor quite what they might meet along the way. Few of them have maps—none have radar.

I admire innovators in any sphere of life because they have the courage to be among the first to try out relatively new and untested ideas. In any field, it is through the early experience and learning of Pathfinders that products and ideas are tested for practicality and that battles are fought against prejudice, habit, the fear of change or the shock of the new. Many Pathfinders (including perhaps some of those described here) will fail. Pathfinders always have a rougher ride than those who follow in the calmer wake of the struggle to prove the worth of their convictions.

I have chosen eight Pathfinders to describe in detail for a variety of reasons. Between them they represent broadly the three main axes of the radar screen model. They also introduce both diverse models of the New Organization and practical approaches to organizational networking while also revealing some recurring themes sufficiently frequently to make me confident that some generalizations can be drawn. Finally, they offer a mix of American, British, mainland European and international company thinking.

None of them can be said to have completed their journeys. Indeed, I believe that all are still in the early stages of them. They are a few steps ahead of most organizations, though, and so these others can benefit from the ideas that they have generated to date and the lessons learned so far, filtering out those elements that will work for them.

Lest anyone feels offended because I did not feature their company, which is even further down the road, I can only apologize for not hearing about their efforts. Of course, there are many others out there who are Pathfinders, too. I hope that someone, somewhere writes about and celebrates *all* of them and lets me know about them, too.

In these very early stages of our understanding of the New Organization and how to make it happen, it behoves us all to be open to learning from whatever quarter.

The Pathfinders are summarized in Box 3.1. The first three, ABB, DPE and Digital follow shortly in this chapter, while the rest appear in each of the next five chapters. Each of them illustrates in some way, but is not exclusively about, the theme of that particular chapter. This selection of Pathfinders represents an insight into where the leading edge of organization thinking is going. Let us peer over this edge together and see what we can learn.

Box 3.1   The Pathfinders

ABB (Chapter 3)	A new, but sophisticated transnational corporation, formed as a result of the merger of large Swiss and Swedish multinationals (Asea & Brown Boveri). ABB's 'network' of small companies is their response to the need to act both globally and locally and to synthesize these two forces.
DPE (Chapter 3)	An international parcel delivery service consisting of 5 'hubs', it is owned by Australian conglomerate Mayne Nickless, collaborating with 198 small, independent businesses round the world that provide its collection and delivery system.
Digital (Chapter 3)	A very advanced model of the networking organization in terms of the sophistication of its electronic linkages and the sheer range of uses to which they are put, both inside the organization world-wide and in many of its customers, research establishments, suppliers and so on. Also, it demonstrates the

	importance of a strong culture—this provides the background rules that mean technology is used well and widely.
Danish biotechnology industry (Chapter 4)	Shows how completely informal, and often unofficial, relationships between individuals in university research, biotechnology companies, their suppliers and their customers stimulates the R&D effort and how the 'rules' of exchange of information operate to prevent any abuse of trust.
World Health Organization, Europe: Healthy Cities Project (Chapter 5)	A unique project that has created multiple networks extending from 35 core cities across Europe, all striving to propagate radical approaches to health improvement within the city. The role of WHO as the orchestrator of the networks and the use of simple soft technologies, such as reports, conferences to accelerate the sharing of learning and best practice, is exemplary.
KWS 2000 (Chapter 6)	A network, potentially, involving every major business and all households in the Netherlands in an ambitious, ten-year plan to make huge reductions in the evaporation of volatile solvents into the Earth's atmosphere.
BP HSE Technology Team (Chapter 7)	A pioneering collaboration venture across several units and businesses within BP to make visible, develop and coordinate the delivery to BP businesses (the customers) of the group's total health, safety and environmental technology expertise.
Benetton (Chapter 8)	This high-profile fashion business orchestrates the activities of its many small, independent suppliers and the independently owned shops throughout the world that carry its name.

PATHFINDER
ABB

Formation

One day during August in 1987, a press conference was called by Percy Barnevik, the Chairman of ASEA, in Stockholm. Financial and business journalists attending assumed it was a relatively routine affair; many did not even bother to turn up. Those present were consequently stunned to hear Percy Barnevik announce that his company, one of Sweden's national institutions, was merging with one of Switzerland's national institutions—the electrical engineering giant, Brown Boveri and that a simultaneous press conference was being held in Zurich.

Preparation for the merger had been conducted with the utmost secrecy. There were already in place comprehensive and well-thought through plans about how the merged company would operate and its key strategic thrusts. What became clear over the months following the formal announcement was that this was not just another merger of two major players. Behind the merger lay the vision of creating a new model of organization that could cope with the competitive demands of the twenty-first century.

Percy Barnevik and his colleagues set out to create a global organization with some very simple, but apparently contradictory, qualities. It had to be an organization that would give true meaning to the cliché that organizations must act both globally *and* locally. It also had to realize the benefits of size while also retaining the assets and attitudes of smallness.

After four years of rationalization, the company was generating $29 billion of sales, employing 214 000 people and had a distribution of revenue and production that was well spread around the world.

Twelve hundred building blocks

The primary design principle was a fundamental belief in radical decentralization. This resulted in an organization consisting of 1200 local companies, each responsible for its profits and losses and each a separate legal and trading entity. One of the remarkable things about these 1200 units is that they have an average size of only 200 employees—tiny in comparison with the monolithic production and organization units that usually characterize the electrical engineering industry. Taking the radical decentralization principle even further, these 1200 units were further divided into more than 4500 profit centres, with an average of only 45 people.

Another fundamental part of the philosophy was to accept and value that most people in the organization would naturally identify with the company at the local level. The 1200 units that employ most of the 214 000 people, therefore, primarily exist to serve their local markets. They do, however, each have designated export markets. The important role of the president of each of these local companies is to be a very efficient profit centre manager, concentrating on serving local and export customers.

Networking the 1200

Given these 1200 building blocks, ABB put in place a number of different structures, roles and processes designed to interconnect the companies in a multiplicity of ways in order to ensure that their resources were most effectively used both locally and globally. This is done by means of two major mechanisms. The global networking 'hub' is a small group of managers, usually only five to ten, who manage what is known internally as a Business Area. These cluster together companies around the world in a particular type of business, having its own market and direct competitors. There is, for example, a power transformers Business Area with 25 factories in 16 countries managed from Mannheim, Germany. Other Business Areas include, for example, instrumentation and electric metering. The Business Area management group is responsible for taking the global view in that particular market.

The second networking hub is at the level of individual countries and is symbolized by the role of the country CEO. The focus of the country CEO is to look at all the resources of ABB (cutting across *all* business areas) within a particular country and to realize synergies between them, while ensuring that ABB as a whole serves the needs of that country and its particular issues and problems to the maximum.

The roles of the Business Area leader and the country CEO are absolutely critical in implementing ABB's vision for they are the two major instruments of what Percy Barnevik has called 'a federation of national companies with intense global coordination'.[1] Very careful thinking has gone into both the design of these roles and assessing the qualities required of managers who fill these roles.

The Business Area leader

The overall purpose of the role is simple. It is to optimize the Business Area's technology base and its overall business activities on a global scale. This means developing, gaining commitment to and championing a global strategy for the companies within that particular Business Area. At a more operational level, this encompasses a range of tasks. Business Area leaders, for example, set cost, quality and other performance standards for their factories world-wide. Within the strategy, they ultimately decide which factories will make what products and which export markets are to be allocated to each company. They also determine how research resource and other expertise is best allocated between the different companies for the benefits of the global business. This involves not only allocating financial resources, but tracking key talent around the world. Each Business Area leader might be responsible for between 60 and 80 high-potential people, constantly looking for ways in which they can be developed and can contribute in different parts of the world. At another level, the Business Area leader is responsible for finding ways of leveraging scale advantages in purchasing.

The ability to operate fluently across different cultures, demonstrating cultural sensitivity while also being able to question and extend perceived boundaries imposed by culture has been seen to be a key quality for these important roles. A second core quality is to be able to create an internal culture of trust and communication among the different companies within the Business Area. It is a fundamental principle that Business Area managers do not own people. Their's is therefore a role that has to operate through influence, inspiration and persuasion. It is clearly a role that requires exceptional leadership qualities, particularly the ability to create and build teams with different nationalities, functions and experience which can realize synergies across their particular locations.

The country CEO

The country CEO's role is primarily to put local interests first. They are there to coordinate the operations of different companies in different Business Areas within the same country. In practice, this involves, most frequently, building an efficient distribution and service network that cuts across product lines and interfacing with major customers, government and media to ensure that ABB is perceived as a local company. It is also their role to coordinate ABB's total approach to a given customer. However, they have to exercise this role while at the same time respecting and actively cooperating with ABB's global strategies. They have to be able to cooperate with Business Area managers while also educating them on the local issues. So their's is a balancing act, a constant synthesizing of the global and the local as the Business Area leaders do, but from a very different perspective.

The Executive Committee

ABB regard it as of no consequence that their small HQ is located in Zurich. The Executive Committee consists of Germans, Swiss, Americans, Dutch and Swedes. They are neither a Swiss company nor a Swedish company. Thomas Gasser, the Deputy CEO, says that it is 'a company with no natural centre. It is a company not with one home but with many homes.'[2] Nevertheless, this small group does have a number of important functions that add further layers of integration and networking to complement those of the country CEOs and the Business Area leaders.

First, they agree and put in place a rigorous and regular standardized reporting system called Abacus. This provides monthly data on all the profit centres that is communicated through electronic data interchange (EDI). ABB's senior executives, used to managing contradictions and paradoxes, have no problems with advocating radical decentralization while at the same time advocating strong, centralized reporting. The Abacus system provides a very clear structure of performance standards that can be applied in a common way throughout Business Areas, countries, companies and profit centres.

Second, the Executive Committee sets the strategy of the company. To quote Thomas Gasser again, 'the group's strategy defines its core activities and goals, identifies key competitive strengths and sets the geographical priorities. The strategy is the frame through which local and international developments can be acted upon in line with long-term goals.'

Its third role is the most important.

Networking processes

Its third role is the provision of a communications infrastructure—not only for EDI, but to ensure efficient telephone and fax communications between the different parts of the group. It is not, however, technology nor financial reporting that really underpins and drives networking within the organization. It is, rather, a range of processes and attitudes that permeates all these senior roles and lies at the heart of ABB's ability to get the most out of its network of 1200 companies. It has evolved a multiple, overlapping approach, systematically understood and systematically applied. It is the ability of those with key roles to articulate, model and be the guardians of these networking processes that is one of ABB's unique attributes.

Fighting national biases

> Problems usually arise when decisions are made on the basis of an often unconscious cultural or national bias. This may happen based on long-accepted and therefore unquestioned practices that are less suitable in a different environment. ABB prides itself on its employees being open-minded about such aspects in their business lives.[3]

In order to help remove such cultural blockages, ABB commits itself to a range of practical actions. They believe strongly in the value of international transfers of key people. They have found that executives with experience of working in three or four countries bring substantial advantages wherever they may be. They also recognize the role of job mobility and transfers in moving ideas and experience from one country to another. It is the Business Area leader in particular who is looking to stimulate this, although, in a different way, the country CEO is looking to widen people's experience by transferring them across different companies within a country.

Another mechanism much favoured within ABB is the assembly of multinational teams to look at problems and come up with solutions. Their experience is that people gain the most and learn the most when they are actually forced to work with people of different nationalities on real issues. Percy Barnevik actually goes so far as to interfere in hiring decisions for such teams if he believes a tendency to drift back into national groupings is occurring. He is insistent, for example, that the small teams at Business Area level are multinational in their constitution.[4]

ABB's senior executives are also avid travellers. There is a strong belief in seeing issues in different countries on the spot and in interacting with people there because it is only through direct contact at a personal level that the necessary networks and alliances are built up across borders. Percy Barnevik estimates that out of about 15000 managers within ABB, there needs to be a core network of about 500 who really can operate in this global manner. The remaining managers do not need to have these particular qualities. It is the travelling 500 who have the critical role of linking companies and other people together.

Continuous exchange of learning

This is another strong set of values that is pushed down the organization into operational levels. *Every* operating unit is expected to *learn* from elsewhere in the group and to *contribute* elsewhere. ABB uses a two-pronged strategy to ensure that this happens.

First, data about the performance of different companies and profit centres is widely available to all parties, particularly within a Business Area. Every unit is able to see how its performance stacks up against the performance of others on key ratios. The Business Area management group ensures that the competition thus engendered is healthy and that its consequences are cooperative activity aimed at improving *everyone's* performance, rather than sustaining a position of winners and losers. Such benchmarking provides a strong incentive for the improvement of performance while also pinpointing areas for application of best practice.

To complement this, both Business Area leaders and country CEOs work on creating mechanisms for facilitating the process of learning and exchange between units. In addition to the permanent linking role of the Business Area teams, there are meetings once or twice a year (known as functional coordination teams) where members of the same function from different companies across the world come together to exchange experiences in an informal manner. While these formal gatherings are carefully designed and do make progress on particular problems and issues, their prime value appears to be in creating personal connections and networks that can then be activated at any time during the remainder of the year. The acid test lies in the regularity of communications that take place on a ongoing basis.[5]

When in doubt, overcommunicate

ABB have learned through bitter experience, particularly in the earlier stages of the merger, that communications do not travel efficiently to all the people who need to hear them. It is a characteristic, perhaps, of these types of organizations that multiple overlapping communication mechanisms are needed to ensure that *all* the nodes of a network are in constant, effective and open communication with each other. There will need to be what many regard as redundant and repetitive communication. Traditionally this is thought to be inefficient; ABB disagrees.

Barriers to progress

ABB is a most challenging example of a company that has set out to create something no one has ever really tried before. The process of creating it is clearly not smooth. It has involved considerable pain in rationalization but also significant difficulties in putting the concept into operation. Percy Barnevik notes a 'strong tendency amongst European managers to be selective about sharing information'.[6] It seems that there are still many deep-seated habits where people's attitudes are in direct conflict with the aspirations of the organization. ABB has also been fortunate: 'We have been able to write our own rules as we went along', says Thomas Gasser. They have found that the demands of the global networking roles, though relatively few in number, mean that it is difficult to find people with the necessary outlook and skills. ABB has actually removed people from some of these roles when it has become apparent that they do not have these qualities.

PATHFINDER
DPE

International parcel delivery

Jean Lo is the Managing Director of a small electronic component manufacturing company in Taipei, Taiwan. She exports her products all over the world. The components are lightweight and thus can be sent by air, meaning a very rapid delivery service for her customers. In the past she has used the major international courier organizations to do this.

However, she has recently been experiencing problems with the customer service provided by these organizations, particularly when anything goes wrong. While she has personal contact with a local office and perhaps a delivery van driver, thereafter, if she wants any information about her consignment, she has to telephone into a central information point in Taiwan. This gets overloaded and can only tell her what is or is not on the central computer.

Recently, therefore, she has been trying a much smaller organization that appears to offer something different. This organization she knows as Document Parcel Express, who are selling her their new international product—DPE.

Jean Lo has decided to try out Document Parcel Express with four of her major international customers. They are located in Nottingham in England, Vienna in Austria, Brussels in Belgium and just outside San Francisco in America. Having got some more information from Jackson Wang, the Customer Service Manager of Document Parcel Express in Taipei, she talks to her customers in these four locations and gives them the name of their local DPE agent, who is responsible for servicing their particular territory. Her customers, in turn, meet their local DPE agent. The customer in San Francisco observes, however, that DPE has no sophisticated infrastructure of electronic communications, owns none of its own aircraft and has no central telephone numbers to dial. He is reassured by his local agent, Robert Gordon of IBC Pacific, that all communications are between the local customer and the local DPE agent, where there is always a personal contact dealing with that account and all aspects of the particular consignment wherever it is going across the world.

A network of independents

DPE has its roots in an Australian-based courier system. They found an increasing demand from their domestic clients to be able to deliver to other countries at high speed. DPE is part of the large Australian security and communications group Mayne Nikless.

DPE's first reaction was that they should purchase and control an international infrastructure, like the big courier companies, but they found no single organization that could provide this apart from the major players. Therefore, they took steps to establish their own hubs. However, when it came to looking for suitable local courier operations to purchase, they could not find any available that came up to their desired standards. It was at this point that they decided to work with the best independent companies to form the DPE International Network.

In 1992, DPE had over 230 agents in its world-wide network. Each of these is a self-employed entrepreneur running their own, independent business with experience of their local area. Each has been invited to join the DPE network based on an assessment of their capabilities made by other members of the network. There are three underlying elements to the relationship between DPE, its fully owned hubs and the 230 agents. By accepting the invitation to join the DPE network, the agents are agreeing (both legally and psychologically) to fulfil a number of conditions.

First, they are buying into a clear-cut vision and philosophy. The common vision of the DPE network is 'to help build an international distribution, door-to-door courier and delivery system as cheaply as possible'. Second, they are buying into a very clear and simple contract that binds them all together. That contract is stated as follows:

> An agent will undertake for and on behalf of the other members of the network, to deliver a consignment *free of charge* within their designated areas, and by doing so expects the same service of others in other parts of the world.

So Jackson Wang in Taipei (who quotes a price to Jean Lo for delivery to Nottingham, England) is paid by her for this service. The consignment gets sent from Taiwan, via scheduled airline services, to be re-routed by the London hub of DPE to Nottingham, England, where James Gallagher, Managing Director of Spatial has agreed to deliver that consignment to Jean Lo's customer free of charge. In other words, no money is exchanged between different agents. The basis of the relationship between agents is not, therefore, a strictly monetary one, but is, nevertheless, a very commercial one in which each network member agrees to get and to keep business on behalf of the others.

Mutual expectations

In order to do this, each new agent agrees to meet some minimum performance criteria and provide a minimum infrastructure of investment to enable the service to work. Each new agent, for example, has to have a certain number of people in place to receive packages 24 hours a day. They have to have an infrastructure of vans that can deliver incoming packages to customers by midday. Each van has to have a radio or telecommunications link back to its office to be able to report any problems in meeting this delivery deadline and they also have to have a system to provide proof of delivery to the customer. In addition, they have to have basic telephone and fax capabilities and be able to nominate key personnel who can be contacted 24 hours a day. They also have to agree to measuring, publishing and disseminating throughout the network their performance against a range of agreed performance standards.

These basic requirements take care of the basic technology and the hardware investment. However, becoming a member of the DPE network also requires commitment to an investment in building relationships among agents and between agents and the hubs. For example, there is a requirement that all agents will meet together twice a year for a working conference. In recent years, these have taken place around the world, being held in Sydney, London, Rome and Istanbul. More detailed meetings of the agents in a particular region associated with a particular DPE hub are held twice a year. The atmosphere of these conferences and meetings is designed to ensure a very open exchange of ideas and information and also to set and reinforce the rigorous performance standards that each member of the network expects of the others. Network members have to be prepared to receive very direct feedback from other agents about perceptions of their performance and problems that have been experienced in dealing with them. The style, therefore, is one both of mutual support and mutual challenge.

At a day-to-day operating level, there is an expectation that direct relationships between agents will be built continuously. Unlike the large players, where all communications go through the hub, DPE requires agents to communicate directly with each other. The hub is primarily a mechanism for routing the physical consignments, as well as for providing a more strategic management overview of a particular regional territory. Therefore, when Jackson Wang's driver in Taipei collects a consignment from Jean Lo's warehouse for delivery to Vienna, the manifest will be made out on return to the office and will be faxed immediately to Nadja Zavratsky at ASAP Spedition, the DPE agent in Vienna, with relevant details of the consignment and its estimated time of arrival. If Nadja spots any problems that might arise from this information, she immediately faxes Jackson Wang to advise him. If there is any big problem, then telephone communications directly between Vienna and Taipei will be the norm, whatever the time of day or night. Using these mechanisms, a network of personal relationships is built up between the network agents as well as between customers in a territory and their local agent.

By getting to understand the different services that different agents in different parts of the world offer, there is enormous scope for reciprocity in terms of ideas, looking out for new business and exchanging learning about problems in different parts of the world. All of this, DPE claim, results in a quality of customer service that is far superior to that provided by the big players. Local knowledge is spread and shared rapidly, providing, DPE believes, a key source of competitive advantage. It is in everyone's interest to sustain this. There is a real risk for each agent of losing the DPE product if they do not perform to standard. Each agent is therefore strongly driven by self-interest in a way that is difficult to reproduce in the wholly owned structure of the larger players.

The advantages for DPE are that they have not had to invest large amounts of money in purchasing a range of agents around the world. They have created a cost-effective structure that can be continuously expanded as it reaches into new territories. They have also avoided the hub becoming a communications blockage for the agents and customers.

For the agents, it enables them to be very attuned to local needs and stay that way, yet be able to operate internationally, too. It also gives them scope for developing their own businesses because they, in effect, have the opportunity to sell new international services to their current customers, but also to develop new customers as a result of delivering consignments to people within their territory that come from other parts of the world. To the customer, the personal, knowledgeable local contact is worth a lot.

How it holds together

Unlike the large courier companies, DPE is not held together by IT systems and advanced communications technology. Their approach is decidedly low-tech, relying primarily on the fax and the telephone. They are currently investing in a relatively simple international computer network that will exchange information between hubs and all agents. This will exchange the information that is currently exchanged by fax, at a higher speed and for less. It will also provide the data on performance standards automatically that is currently generated by each agent, as well as making provisions for the future in terms of expanded capacity.

The key thing about this new technology is that it is purely for internal use. It does not replace the personal interface with the customer, but is, instead, designed to *support* the individual agent's relationships with the customers and make individual agents' lives easier. Nevertheless, it is a sobering thought that DPE could not work as it does at present without the simple technology of the fax—a relatively recent invention. The core of DPE's internal integration, however, is provided by a carefully nurtured network of direct person-to-person relationships, coupled to clear, shared goals and values.

Developing the business

The nature of this 'psychological contract' between the agents and with the hub also produces a very interesting mechanism through which DPE develops and changes. As James Gallagher of Spatial points out, 'amongst 230 independent people there will always be very differing views. You can't force them to go in a direction that they don't want to go in. And even then you probably can't get them all going in the same direction.' This poses interesting questions about how you develop and implement strategy in such an organization.

The way that it is happening is by individual agents trying things out. They try things by first selling a new service locally and then selling it on to other agents. Initially this may happen in a haphazard way. For example, one such product came out of a small group at one of the conferences who decided to try it out on an experimental basis. The small group worked among themselves to refine the idea and then in turn made it available to others within the wider network. Strategy, in this model, emerges, as Henry Mintzberg[7] would describe it, rather than being planned. It builds on identifying those people within the network who are motivated by a particular idea and are prepared to make it happen. In this sense, strategy becomes just as much a role of the individual agent as it does of the board of DPE. It becomes owned as much by the elements of the network (the agents) as it is by the centre.

DPE's future

Does the network organization model DPE has developed threaten the supremacy of the major players? James Gallagher believes not, in that the model has some self-limiting factors. He feels, for example, that it would be difficult to continue the personal relationships between agents if the numbers got too much larger. The other route to expansion is obviously the growth in the size of individual agents' businesses. However, once again, he feels that those who participate in this scheme actually like the fact that they are *not* very large businesses, because they are thereby able to preserve a sense of personal control, personal service and personal involvement. The most likely scenario therefore seems to be that DPE, while having some capacity for growth, will maintain itself as a niche player with a relatively small market share, but one that is, nevertheless, an irritant for the major players and one which, by its very nature, will be difficult for the major players to obliterate using the normal tactic of acquisition.

DPE gives us some very interesting elements. The truly independent (not franchised) nature of its entrepreneur agents and the large degree of interdependence between them has some unique characteristics. Its use of simple technologies and soft networking, building direct personal connections by phone, by fax and by conferencing shows how far you can go without necessarily investing in more sophisticated technology. It also clearly articulates the expectations that each element has of the others in terms of individual performance standards, communications and collective goals. It understands very well the principles of reciprocity and the valuing of differences. It is also learning how to keep renewing itself by evolving strategy processes appropriate to a structure of 230 autonomy-loving prima donnas.

PATHFINDER
DIGITAL

The free flow of information creates excitement, motivation and enthusiasm and helps unify the company . . . it is a strong internal catalyst and a powerful competitive tool.

Ken Olsen, Digital Equipment Corporation, Annual Report 1986

History

'We never designed Digital as a networking organization . . . it just happened', says Lutz Reuter, an internal organization consultant within Digital.[8] Well, if it just happened, it created one of the most advanced examples of a high-tech networking organization so far. What has 'just happened' over only 30 years is the creation of a company with revenues in 1991 of $14 billion and 126 000 employees, 40 000 of whom are in Europe. In the 'eighties it achieved six-fold growth in Europe.

That this remarkable accident has come about is in no small measure due to the particular combination of characteristics and demands on Digital as it has evolved. It operates in the computing industry where, particularly in the last 10 or 15 years, rapid product life cycles have been the order of the day. Digital's hardware products, on average, only have a shelf-life of between 9 and 18 months. At the same time, the very nature of the company's business has changed substantially, with the result that it has radically reorganized every seven years or so. It started off as a 100 per cent hardware company. It then began to move itself forwards again by talking about itself as a 'solutions' company. Beyond that it talked about becoming a 'service' company. As the unit prices of hardware tumbled, service became a commodity that in many instances could be bought together with the hardware. The service concept is now evolving even further, with the company emphasizing that it is a 'consultancy' company, helping organizations to analyse their businesses and the role of IT within their future businesses, then implement IT-based solutions effectively. The result is a gradually shifting spectrum of focus and activity, with hardware in 1991 accounting for only 40 per cent of revenue.

Another unique characteristic of this industry—Digital in particular—is the youth of its employees. Digital's employees are mostly in their mid thirties, a population for whom 'hierarchy doesn't stick', says Reuter. Many insiders and observers have likened Digital to a university, saying that it is run like one. Its culture provides the characteristics of individual autonomy, freedom of thought, free flow and exchange of information and ideas. It backs this up with a formidable capability in hard network technology. This must also be due to the fact that it is itself in the high-tech business. It is swarming with people who have as good a knowledge as anyone in the world of the technological possibilities. This deep technical base is strongly reinforced by Digital's commitment to engineering and R&D. As David Skyrme, a research programme manager with Digital in the UK puts it:

> Digital has the peer-to-peer networking technology it enjoys because it has essentially been a human peer-to-peer networking company from its inception.[9]

Advanced communications technology

These factors have been important in building up one of the most comprehensive electronic communications networks in the world. Every employee world-wide has direct access to some kind of terminal. Over 40 000 computers are connected to the integrated network, a third handling text only and others being PCs and work stations. These terminals are capable of exchanging text and graphics (and shortly speech) information. Approximately 15 per cent of employees also have terminals or PCs in their homes. Many employees who travel away a lot from their prime locations carry a small, portable computer that enables them to plug into the world-wide communications network from any other distant location. Digital rents permanent time and band widths on communications satellites and other forms of direct connection between major locations across the world.

E-mail, videotex and an electronic conferencing system (VAX Notes) are at the heart of the exchange process. Videotex communicates company information and news to all employees. Within VAX Notes there is a myriad of different kinds of 'bulletin boards' or computer conferences that employees can use to inform colleagues and other work groups of their needs and their offerings. Up to 1500 'open access' conferences (literally anyone can contribute) and many more 'closed' conferences, limited to registered participants, are on the go at any one time. One third of all employees use the system regularly in their work. These computer conferences are used, for example, when people are involved in the development of new products. There are stories of messages about technical problems going out on the bulletin board around the world, responses being received from different locations, new solutions to problems being found within days and new products emerging months earlier than would otherwise be possible as a result of this system. Frequently, these are developed by people who have never met each other and of whom half are sleeping while the other half work. The ability to send pictures (both in black and white and in colour) also provides an enormously important extra dimension in terms of the ease of communicating ideas, particularly in technical areas.

Not only has each employee access to the network, but they can also communicate via 'gateways' with a large number of customers, suppliers, universities, R&D establishments and other outside information sources. This enables, for example, sophisticated production planning and just-in-time systems to work through EDI as well as customers being able to access product and pricing information on a wide range of third-party software packages that run on Digital hardware. It is also testament to the openness with which information is exchanged and received and the ability of the system to act as an antenna into the outside world for new ideas and new trends. It is said that during the Tiananmen Square riots in Peking, Digital received information about what was going on before the world's media. The messages came via those people on the spot who knew how to link into the system, a testament to the power of electronic networks to reach the parts others cannot reach.

The social side of technology

An important early lesson was that the technology affected and required related management processes. One of the ways in which this has happened is through the development of some special roles. One such role is that of the conference moderator. Computer conferencing, when not properly managed, easily became unwieldy and the system got jammed with excess and out-of-date information. The moderator acts as a kind of electronic chairman for a computer conference, ensuring that the topic does not drift from its purpose, that the rules of fair play are followed, relevant people are aware of its progress and all adhere to relevant legal and ethical practice. Another important role is that of 'linkers', who, when questions are raised, point people to areas of the same or other conferences where answers or debates have or are taking place.

David Skyrme also relates how standards of etiquette and norms of behaviour have evolved to make such electronic conferencing work effectively. For instance, individuals are expected to contribute their knowledge to a debate openly and willingly, if necessary arguing vigorously for a position, but never to the point where, or in such a way that, it can be perceived as criticism of the person whose ideas are being challenged.

On a more general level, he cites some of the cultural norms that seem to be essential, such as a degree of informality, a belief that coordinating and gaining ideas from others is better than going it alone, a strong sense of responsibility for helping fellow employees and a high degree of self-regulation of the network. Many of these human qualities then become ascribed to the networking technology itself in the metaphors that people start using to describe what is happening. They talk about E-mail messages passing back and forth as 'conversations' or 'talking to them about that'. A dispersed group working on a problem via VAX Notes talk about 'sharing ideas' or 'having an extended meeting' and the increasing knowledge storehouse that is constantly being built up and continually drawn upon, recorded within the systems, is referred to as 'organizational memory'.[10]

The technological system, therefore, enables both the unfettered sharing of information and of applications. There is, without doubt, an inbuilt level of overlap, duplication and redundancy, but this is of no concern to Digital. Their prime objective is to make the sharing of information free from boundaries or difficulties.

Another critical role that has emerged is what Lutz Reuter calls 'fourth-generation super users'. These are secretaries who have become so skilled in how to operate the system that they are able to make world-wide connections both within and outside Digital without any difficulty and can also use all the sophisticated software applications with which different kinds of information can be generated and transmitted around the world.

Technology affects structure

The drive to integrate technology in order to make information accessible anywhere has had some very powerful effects on the subsequent structure and integration of the organization itself. One effect has been that the traditional role of middle managers becomes more or less redundant. Digital's organization has been built on a philosophy of radical delegation, coupled with some tight on-line controls. It was observed in the early days how easy it was to start the process of delegation, but, at the same time, impose tighter controls in unnecessarily wide areas, thus restricting people's autonomy and defeating some of the very objectives of instituting access to information.

Digital has, in the past, operated what it calls a complex network of interdependent business units where many people will have up to four or five 'bosses'. In the most recent evolution of the European organization, the core role is what they call the 'entrepreneur'. This is a person whose purpose is directed towards the customer, their job being to 'pull out' of the organization the resources needed to satisfy that customer. The aim is that all such resource people have a 'customer-facing' attitude. The entrepreneur has revenue and profit accountability and is, in effect, running their own business.

The role of senior managers (now many fewer in number and restyled with the title 'coach') then becomes to provide the supportive environment and strategic infrastructure within which entrepreneurs can succeed. Their role is to intervene—as would a sports team's trainer—to bring their team up to its peak performance potential, but they do not have formal line authority over the entrepreneurs. Indeed, taken to its extremes there is very little exercising of direct line authority within Digital. Most roles are built on the premise that individuals and groups need to influence and coordinate the activities of others over whom they have little or no formal authority. Essentially individuals and groups agree contracts for goals and objectives and are then held responsible for delivering these. This provides strong commitment as well as clear and binding account-ability.

The culture and its consequences

Whether the culture of the organization came before or after its technological and business development is difficult to disentangle. The technology, the management style and the culture are deeply interdependent and intertwined. At root, there has always been a strong vision and value about information sharing which preceded the technology but which technology has enabled. However, as each phase of technological development and business development has been gone through, this has, in turn, led to a challenging of the values and norms that characterized each stage. Many have survived but also many evolve and change as the organization develops. Hierarchy, functional specialization, the roles of middle management, organizations as stable entities, the very nature of power and authority—all these fundamental tenets of the traditional organization have been challenged and found wanting. Instead, the culture that has emerged is one strongly focused on self-organization, on semi-autonomous groups and teams tied together by well-defined communications and task interdependencies. Pier Carlo Falotti, President and CEO of Digital Europe, expressed the culture simply and memorably through the 'mind map' shown in Figure 3.1 which is widely circulated within the company.

The role of management has been to provide the power of vision (defining the what but not the how) and to 'enable' knowledge workers to be more successful by cutting through or revising policies or processes that get in their way. Measurement has been radically simplified. Very little detail gets measured corporately. The accent is on measuring the whole and not the detail. There is an

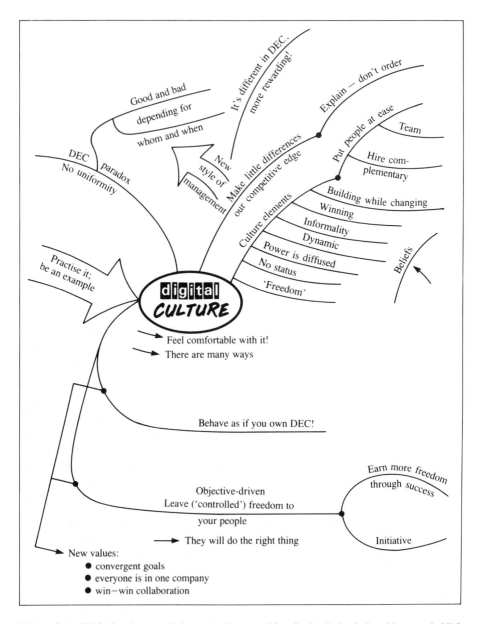

Figure 3.1 Digital culture 'mind map'. (Source: Pier Carlo Falotti, President and CEO, Digital Equipment Corporation International (Europe).)

acute external focus, an awareness that both people and the technology should be used to look out for weak signals of change in the external environment. The culture is one of intended ambiguity or organized chaos—characteristics that can be extremely difficult for new people joining the organization.

People newly hired by the organization are coached or supervised so they learn about how to get things done within Digital. For many newcomers, there is a radical form of culture shock that is now understood far better than in the early days. People learn that the route to personal and organizational success is intimately linked to the degree to which they can persuade others to accept and implement their ideas. It seems a fundamentally important part of Digital's networking organization that it allows and enables dedicated and persistent knowledge workers to pursue their innovative ideas.

Having said all this, the rapid growth during the 'eighties brought a dilution of the original networking culture and bureaucracy started to creep in, stifling initiative. The new entrepreneur structure is designed to reassert the guiding principles of the founders. All of this creates an organization that has been described as manic depressive. It is an organization suffused with enormous energy and, at times, emotion. It is an organization that is enormously fast-moving with high levels of trust, an intentional ambiguity of rules and a regard for people and their contributions. However, the people very much have to stand on their own feet. They have to be able to handle the lack of rules and have the confidence to involve and inspire others to follow their paths. Every individual, in some sense, needs to be a leader.

The density of information flow also creates some singular pressures. For one thing, people *cannot* say 'I didn't know about it'. This, therefore, places a burden of responsibility on all individuals that is frequently lacking in many other organizations. It does also mean that there is information overload, something that people have to learn to cope with. It means that, at times, there are so many relationships that have to be managed in order to make things happen that the organization becomes stuck and individuals become depressed at their apparent powerlessness. Life can become very intense as the complexity has to be dealt with and consensus has to be sought among many parties. Yet, although this can, at times, be a frustrating and lengthy process, once it is achieved, the organization can move with a startling rapidity that is heady and exciting for those taking part. It is a paradox that although in many ways it is a stressful organization, it is also an organization that has very low staff turnover. This is at centre of it all because it makes exciting demands of people and gives them enormous scope to realize their ideas and ambitions.

The mature Pathfinder

Digital is a very mature Pathfinder in that it has at least ten years' experience of operating a complicated high-tech global communications system and learning how best to use that technology as a tool to support and extend the networks of personal relationships on which the company is based.

Indeed, it was the creation of Digital's early culture, aimed at preserving the innovativeness of the small company that, along with its enormous technical capability, enabled it to benefit so rapidly from the new communications technologies. Digital teaches us that hard networking technology cannot create organizational networking. The New Organization is built on a foundation of widespread social networking, supported by a culture of information sharing. It is only if hard technologies, build on such foundations that a quantum leap in breadth and effectiveness can be taken.

What Digital also demonstrates is the need to be managing the relationship between people and the communications technologies constantly to ensure that they remain useful tools rather than frustrating or absorbing diversions. It is this comprehensive and intimate intertwining of people, technology and culture that is fascinating for some, horrifying for others.

References

1 Taylor, William (1991) 'The Logic of Global Business: an interview with ABB's Percy Barnevik', *Harvard Business Review*, March–April, pp 92–105.
2 Gasser, Thomas (1991) 'Managing without Boundaries: the challenge to business', speech to Annual Conference of the European Forum for Management Development, The Hague, June.
3 Gasser, Thomas (1991) ibid.
4 Taylor, William (1991) ibid.
5 Taylor, William (1991) ibid.
6 Taylor, William (1991) ibid.
7 Mintzberg, Henry (1988) 'Crafting Strategy', *McKinsey Quarterly*, Summer, pp 71–90.
8 Reuter, Lutz (1991) Talking in a joint workshop, 'The Networking Organization: fact or fantasy', European Forum for Management Development Conference, The Hague, June.
9 Skyrme, David (1992) 'Knowledge Networking—creating wealth through people technology', *The Intelligent Enterprise*, January, pp 9–15.
10 Skyrme, David (1992) ibid.

Chess

Most of you are probably familiar with chess pieces that stand on a chequered board. Even if you are not, suffice to say that each kind of piece is proscribed in terms of where it is allowed to move. Pawns, the lowliest of pieces, are very limited in their options. The only piece that is allowed to move freely is the queen, which can move imperiously upwards, downwards, sideways and diagonally.

One of the best images arising from the rules of chess is that if a pawn reaches the other side of the board, it can turn into a queen. Perhaps in this image is a clue to one of the underlying dreams of networking: turning pawns into queens. If all the pieces on the board were queens, they would have total freedom of movement. Imagine that there are many games of chess going on, perhaps in the same room, as in a grand masters tournament. Imagine that suddenly all these chess boards are connected together and that all the pieces can move freely throughout the expanded territory.

Part II
Growing the culture of
organizational networking

Introduction

Organizational networking, as the frameworks and examples covered so far demonstrate, is both a wide-ranging set of tools and an attitude of mind. If it is to truly become part of the organization's culture ('the way we do things round here') and to produce lasting benefits, it has to be grown and nurtured over a long period of time as one would tend any exotic plant to encourage it to flower. How to grow such a culture is the theme of Part II.

Implanting organizational networking requires that you grow five main roots to feed the process and ensure that you benefit from the prizes of the New Organization (Figure 4.1 summarizes these). How to go about developing each one in your organization is covered in the following five chapters.

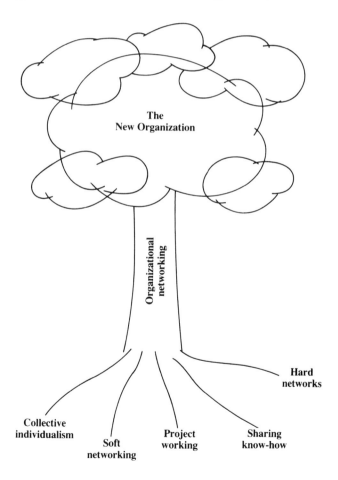

Figure 4.1   The roots of organizational networking © Colin Hastings, New Organisation Consulting. (This diagram may be reproduced freely with due acknowledgement.)

4
Collective individualism—how to turn knowledge workers into effective networkers

PATHFINDER
The Danish biotechnology industry

Exotic organizations

When I first heard the name Kristian Kreiner, he was described to me as a 'Professor of exotic organizations' at the Copenhagen Business School. His unit, the Institute of Organization and Industrial Sociology, was conducting, among other things, a study into the ways that high-tech firms collaborate across European boundaries in such programmes as EUREKA and ALVEY, sponsored by the EC Commission. One aspect of the study Kristian Kreiner carried out, with his colleague Majken Schultz, looked into some of the key innovation processes that characterize the Danish biotechnology industry. They have been kind enough to allow me to summarize what they found as given in their paper 'Crossing the Institutional Divide'.[1]

While much publicity has been given to formal strategic alliances between firms as ways of gaining access to external know-how and resources, Kreiner and Schultz found that much more pervasive mechanisms of collaboration were being pursued by means of what they called 'the unpaved paths in the undergrowth of less formalised, personalised networks'. In particular, they found a web of collaborative relationships between very different kinds of institutions. On the one hand there were people working in large pharmaceutical companies and, on the other, people working in very small research-orientated spin-off firms, often started up by people coming out of large pharmaceutical companies or universities. Last, there were people working within university and government-sponsored research institutions. While it has become a cliché to talk about the differences of culture between large companies, small companies and universities and to stress the difficulties that people from these different backgrounds have in working with each other, Kreiner and Schultz found that, on the contrary, there were very few barriers to a widespread informal exchange of favours and services between all parties, which in some cases developed into longer term joint projects.

Many of these connections between people in such institutions are clearly driven by the nature of the biotechnology industry itself. First, it has a highly cross-disciplinary nature. It draws heavily on biology, chemistry and the other natural sciences, but also very much on applied engineering disciplines, which provide a crucial contribution to the commercial exploitation of the results. Exploitation frequently requires new kinds of instruments, equipment and production technology. Thus, it is not only pharmaceutical companies and researchers but also manufacturers of production and test equipment, as well as the users of such equipment, that form the extended network.

A second aspect of biotechnology is that it is truly a frontier science. It catches the imagination of researchers, managers, economists and politicians alike. It is characterized by a tremendous sense of optimism, a belief that everything and anything is possible. It is this widespread shared sense of mission that provides people in different types of institutions with a common set of interests and motivations.

Occasions and opportunities

Kreiner and Schultz found that one type of interaction within the extended network was what they called 'need driven'. Quite simply, this involved one person requesting a favour or service from somebody else. For example, one person would provide some speciality chemicals and another person would ask for a spare part for a machine that had broken down at a crucial time.

However, beyond these specifically initiated requests, the researchers found that there were many other occasions on which people came together. Even in the needs-initiated interactions, they found that when people met and talked, they would go beyond the specific purpose of the conversation to exchange gossip, current ideas, work plans and concerns. Keeping in touch was important. Other occasions where people met included formalized research relationships (contracted research or collaborative research projects), at conferences and other professional meetings, at social and private gatherings (many of these people had worked and studied together over a large number of years) and in public bodies (such as research councils or government taskforces). Other occasions were engineered by a third party to bring two people together. For instance, a chemical company's salesperson was able to make two customers aware of certain links in their R&D activities that subsequently led to a direct contact between the two people.

Perhaps the most interesting aspect of the researchers' conclusions was that most of the perceived benefits to emerge from these contacts came from accidental opportunities spotted in the course of the general sharing of information. In fact, their observation is that these accidentally arising opportunities are a more fertile breeding ground for real cooperation than the more formally directed ones, such as strategic alliances and joint ventures.

The igniting idea

The question then arises as to what makes people who are sharing information suddenly click over some particular item, which then develops into a more systematic process of collaboration. What the researchers called the 'igniting idea' would usually stir in both parties a sense of scientific excitement as, at the same time, each party becomes aware of a high potential for contributing to the field.

Thus, the creation of opportunities for people to link externally becomes a very important mechanism that organizations can use to stimulate innovation within their own organizations. One of the difficulties people frequently encounter who are wanting, for instance, to go to conferences or visit other companies, is that they are asked to justify in advance the benefits they are going to gain from it. Clearly, a change of mind set is required here. As the researchers remark, 'It is the unplanned way in which the blending (of ideas) is done which may be especially conducive to innovation. The opportunity-driven interaction almost by necessity lets pieces of information, ideas and gossip travel to places where they are neither asked for nor, according to conventional wisdom, relevant.'

Crystals of collaboration

From these small beginnings starts a more complicated process. Frequently, a single idea may develop purely between two people. Equally, the web of collaboration may widen as new people come in at various stages to contribute to the development of a specific element. As Kreiner and Schultz put it,

> one way of capturing the development process of crystallised collaboration is to see the parties involved in collaboration not as the original individuals encountering and connecting, but as these individuals *and* their respective networks. The original accidental contact brings hitherto separate parts of the field to mesh, temporarily reshuffling links of communication and collaboration. Through this, highly unlikely partners oftentimes find themselves sharing projects that nobody would consciously have designed . . . When occasionally shared projects emerge, interactions crystallise into somewhat more durable, committing forms of relationships. . . . While they exist, these crystallised relationships act as 'centres of gravity', in the sense that they seem to attract more researchers. . . . Being part of one such crystal of collaboration, does not seem to prevent (in terms of time or loyalty) anybody from participating fully in the current (wider) stream of interaction.

Beyond the barter economy

The notion of the barter economy captures some of the essence of these interactions between people. Many exchanges take place in different currencies. Organic material, laboratory tests, chemicals, instruments, access to laboratory facilities, research assistance, travelling tickets, literature searches, results, specialized knowledge and experiences are all widely traded, frequently not in an openly negotiated manner but clearly in a systematic and recurrent way.

However, the exchanges are not simple tit-for-tat type exchanges; people will give without receiving an instantaneous exchange. Indeed, the researchers found that there was very little concern for the immediate return of the favour and very few precautions taken to ensure that reciprocation would come eventually. The whole process was based very much on a sense of trust that others would reciprocate in some way at some time.

It was this observation that led the researchers to go beyond the barter economy model and suggest that the whole process is much better characterized as *sharing* rather than *exchanging*. They point out that on the traditional barter model,

> when rivals (trade) . . . the value of the additional information acquired in trade is assumed to exceed the loss in value of the information shared . . . it is taken for granted that the act of sharing knowledge or information depreciates its value. . . . However the kind of information in our case is different from know-how and knowledge: in our study the kind of information is more like loose ideas and 'inspirations' which are a long way from any application. Thus their immediate value as such is low, and the loss from sharing it is low too. To the extent that other researchers can be motivated to work on these ideas and inspirations, the value of the idea may rapidly increase, for the benefit of both parties.

The unwritten code of conduct

Clearly such a process of exchange is open to exploitation and corruption. Many organizations would be very nervous about encouraging people to trade information in this manner for fear of how it could be misused. What the researchers found was an unwritten, but surprisingly sophisticated, code of conduct that had grown up within the biotechnology field, which regulated people's behaviour and was quite clearly understood, though seldom overtly articulated.

The first element was a strong realization among the different parties that they all wanted to stay at the frontier of research and development. They realized that they could not do this without keeping very up to date with the current stream of information and ideas. Networking seems to be the only way to obtain such frontier-type information. Aspiring to making a contribution on the frontier also strongly hinges on gaining the assistance of other people in terms of good advice or bright ideas. Therefore, both individuals and organizations realized that if they are to stay competitive in terms of their careers and in terms of their performance in the market-place, they must operate on the frontier. Operating on the frontier requires cooperation. Therefore, in order to compete, they must cooperate.

Kreiner and Schultz found a number of ways in which companies and individuals dealt with the paradoxes of this situation. How do you resolve the issue of getting your product to the market first without anyone else knowing about it when you know that others probably *have* to know something about it to achieve this. As they observe, 'indiscretion is exactly what networking entails!' They found that, in general, such 'indiscretions' were both tolerated and unofficially legitimated, but never publicly condoned or even discussed. They quote one research director who observed. 'I only hope they (the researchers) use sound judgement'. It is not the indiscretion itself as such that requires sound judgement, but, instead, knowing *what* information to leak and, especially, to *whom* it should be leaked. Therefore, anybody found responsible for leaking information that subsequently was illegitimately exploited by outsiders would be severely punished for their poor judgement.

Another prerequisite for a successful system was the intangible factor of trust. For those involved in the network, trust meant that 'entrusted knowledge would not be misused, stolen or leaked to third parties. Anybody being accused of such an act would rapidly become a leper in the field. Illegitimate use of shared information was considered *the* deadly sin of networking. They go on to explain the point in more detail.

> The ultimate signal of trustworthiness may indeed be the act of volunteering proprietary knowledge oneself, thereby seemingly making a personal investment in the possibility for a future trust-born relationship. This symbolism may, in fact, explain the ultimate sanction of isolation elicited against too 'discreet' researchers: networking with such persons would be too risky, even if otherwise attractive and relevant.

Thus the process of networking has to be in some sense self-regulating. However, there are ways in which the management in these organizations contributed indirectly to providing and assisting with this self-regulation process. Their job was to raise the awareness and understanding of researchers to the wider issues that their behaviour involved. So, for example, it would be made very clear that researchers were expected to protect the intellectual property of the company while also recognizing that they would be exchanging confidential information informally. Making these paradoxes explicit forces the researchers consciously to balance considerations involved in making their choices about what information is appropriate to share and what is not appropriate to share. Likewise, researchers have to have an understanding both of the short-term objectives that they face and also of the longer term company strategy and objectives. Part of exercising 'sound judgement' would be to balance the requirements of the long term against the imperatives of the short term—another difficult balancing act.

Both/and, not either/or

Similar processes and norms no doubt exist in many other environments. Silicon Valley in California, Route 128 in Boston, Massachusetts and the Thames Valley corridor in England, are all geographic areas where innovatory companies have clustered like bees in a hive. Kreiner and Schultz's significant contribution has been to describe what to most people remains invisible—the underlying processes and rules that create a sense of purposeful order within the apparent chaos.

The study also gives some important insight into the motivations and skills of so-called knowledge workers who thrive on being given trust and autonomy as well as the personal recognition of contributing, while also recognizing that collective networking processes can provide the means to their own and to the organization's goals.

I find that many people have great difficulty with the idea that we should be encouraging both individualism *and* collectivism simultaneously. They see them as opposites. The Japanese understand better than westerners that in complicated situations, such black or white, either/or thinking is inappropriate. It is one of the challenges of the New Organization that we will all need to learn to think in 'both/and' terms and to master the art of living with paradoxes. Perhaps Kreiner and Schultz help us to understand the underlying rationale for pursuing both. At its root, the New Organization will be built around creating an environment that attracts and motivates the new knowledge workers. The skilled individuals will realize that they can best do that by looking for areas where their needs link with those of the organization and will realize, too, that many of their needs can *only* be met by cooperating with others.

From people as instruments for organizations to organizations as instruments for people.   Roald Nomme, Alusuisse

1   Individual barriers to networking

Whereas only 20 years ago the cost of materials was the major element in product costs, its contribution to the total cost has been declining dramatically. Electronic components, for instance, actually cost very little. The major cost to be recouped in many services products nowadays is the R&D that has gone into their creation and refinement. The know-how component in any company's product or service is increasing rapidly. This means that organizations rely more and more on the so-called knowledge workers to bring their talent into the organizations and thereafter to contribute it and develop it.

Need for autonomy

Research and experience demonstrate that autonomy (the space to make decisions and get on with what needs to be done) is much valued by many such organization members.[2] Yet this conflicts directly with the need to share information and responsibility and to work with others, which is central to organizational networking.

There is also a direct conflict between the desire of individuals to have this autonomy (which requires of them a very pro-active belief in their ability to make things happen) and the reality which is that many of them, for a variety of reasons, are not able to exercise such pro-activity. They find themselves inhibited by both visible and invisible forces that stop them from crossing traditional boundaries of function, level or location in order to do what they need to do. The shadow of hierarchy from parents, schools and early work experience is long. The organization will therefore need to accelerate people's ability to operate effectively in this environment.

Need for recognition

Apart from the desire for autonomy, knowledge workers are also very strongly driven by their need for recognition.[3] In the past, much of this came from the status that level, function and other symbols gave them within the organizational context. Yet, in order to make networking work, such status symbols need to be removed and barriers between professions need to be broken down in order to create multidisciplinary teams. These requirements of networking do present individuals with difficult inner conflicts.

Another kind of conflict arises when people strongly identify with their area of professional expertise. They have learned over time that they gain recognition by visibly demonstrating that expertise to other people. When dealing with clients (be they internal or external), this attitude of mind most frequently creates a product-orientated or selling style of interaction with the client, where the 'expert' is showing the client what they have available in terms of techniques, technologies or expertise. Such experts have great difficulty in truly listening and seeking to understand clients' needs. They can only frame the world in terms of what they have to offer rather than what the client actually wants. The mores and assumptions of some parts of the professional world also act more insidiously where professionals actually hide their expertise from the client, believing that this in some way is private knowledge of which the client need not be aware. This has operated, for instance, in the legal and medical professions who have felt little obligation in the past to explain to their clients what they are doing and how they are coming to their conclusions. The client-orientated attitude and sharing of information ethos implicit in the network way of working, is a quite fundamentally different orientation to professional relationships. Thus many people who have always worked in the traditional professional environment find it very difficult either to accept or execute their work in the New Organization.

Individualism

A final barrier to effective organizational networking lies in the western cult of individualism, in particular among men. Asking for help is seen and experienced as an admission of failure, while the person achieving the impossible by himself, is seen as a hero. The rugged individualist, maverick or intrapreneur as the source of much organizational innovation has been idolized as a stereotype by too many managers—a kind of Clint Eastwood of the managerial world. Several studies reveal that, in reality, these successful 'individualists' get things done not alone, but through their ability to mobilize other people.[4]

A sense of loss

In the transition process, people have a sense of loss where traditional boundaries between specialisms are reduced, where hierarchical roles are removed and where expert relationships vis-à-vis clients and suppliers are eliminated. In addition, where traditional functional groups break down and professionals are given autonomy to access other disciplines directly, individuals appear to lose the recognition they have traditionally received from peers within their own area of expertise. They have not traditionally received recognition from other professional groups. Overt or covert rivalry and competitiveness between such groups has more frequently been the norm.

So nobody should underestimate what individuals may have to let go of as well as what they may gain by adopting the New Organization. Does it mean that they have to let go of individualism and the desire for autonomy? Does it mean that they have to let go of the luxury of being told what to do and, instead, take responsibility for making judgements and making things happen by themselves? Does it mean that they have to let go of the status that comes via functional expertise and in its place take a client- or a broad business-orientated viewpoint? Does it mean that conventional symbols of status are now irrelevant and that something else has to be put in its place? These problems cannot be simply resolved with a yes or a no. The New Organization will demand that people can answer both yes and no, that they can be autonomous at times and cooperative and let go of some forms of status but acquire new ones that are not linked to hierarchy but to contribution.

Understanding the underlying paradoxes of knowledge workers' motivation and the factors that stimulate and inhibit their contribution is going to be central. The New Organization is designed partly around their needs. Personnel people in particular will need to do some radical, fresh thinking to replace their traditional practices, many of which sustain the status quo of the command and control model. Organizations that really come up with fresh, clear policies and programmes for *attracting, developing, rewarding* and *retaining* knowledge workers will create for themselves a significant competitive edge. New Organization ideas form one part of their new tool kit. At least in the foreseeable future, considerable training and development in the skills of collective individualism will need to take place in the workplace, for it will not have been learned anywhere else. This, along with growing the roots of Organizational Networking, will provide the strategy for overcoming individuals' barriers to networking.

2   Organizational barriers to networking

Some of the barriers lie within the individuals themselves, but many lie within the organization's culture, systems and processes and need to be addressed by senior managers and personnel people.

Permission

Many people describe a sense of risk or fear of crossing organizational boundaries. One project manager said, 'If I go and talk to another department, I always get the sense that they will ask me why I am coming to talk to them, and that doesn't exactly make me feel welcome'. Another manager said, 'I went to another department to ask for some vital information and the reply I got was "why do you want it?" instead of "yes, how can we help"'. Yet another person from an oil company said, 'I feel I somehow have to get "permission" to cross boundaries, whether to other departments or up the line. I know at a rational level that this is ridiculous but nevertheless this is how I feel and that inhibits me. I'm still afraid of upsetting the boss. Its absurd.'

The exclusive club

A second organizational barrier is the 'exclusive club' syndrome. This came up particularly strongly in one company where there were very clearly different kinds of mafias and closed circles. A lot of networking took place within the boundaries of these circles, which were certainly not permeable. Here was a very clear example of the old boys network where others felt it very difficult to break in. Kevin Barham, of Ashridge Management Research Group, puts the problem well: 'There is a danger that networks can degenerate into in-groups. By excluding other groups of people, they may inhibit the very flow of information that is their *raison d'être*.' Expatriate managers from the parent country may, for example, develop their own network, which keeps out local managers. Ericsson, for example, recognizes that its network has been mainly Swedish in composition and that in future it will be necessary to bring many more local people into the firm's global network.

In companies where managers have built up relationships over the years, newcomers may find it difficult to become members of the network. Unilever is aware of this problem. In recognition of the tighter recruitment market for graduates brought about by demographic changes, it aims to hire more mid-career managers. It realizes that such people will need help to enter the network and assigns to each mid-career entrant a mentor whose job it is to familiarize them with Unilever's way of working. The company also runs a three-day seminar for mid-career recruits on 'Undertaking How Unilever Works'.[5]

'Busyness'

Another invisible barrier was described by a project manager in an engineering consultancy. She was discussing how she felt about networking as the company tried to move towards this concept.

> It's fine with my colleagues and even those in other parts of the organization and outside, but I find it really difficult with senior management. Whenever I ring up senior managers I get the feeling they are in a hurry, that they want me to get off the telephone. I just pick up the vibes which say 'I'm a very busy person. Can't you ask someone else?' That is not conducive to quality networking. And so in practice I don't bother to try to use the senior management network.

Such feelings are surprisingly commonplace. Some of them stem from very real experiences, where the crossing of a boundary has been met with some kind of rebuff or rejection. The shadow of hierarchy and functionalism does indeed run wide and deep.

3   Learning how to be effective

Michael Maccoby's fascinating study of the underlying motivations of knowledge workers, called 'Why Work . . . leading the new generation', showed that, after recognition for their expertise and contribution, people's own personal development came second in the league table of motivators.[6]

The problem with much formal development that takes place in knowledge organizations is that it is still primarily aimed at enhancing and reinforcing the individual's specialist expertise. The lessons of the New Organization suggest that this emphasis will need to change. Professional expertise will be learned on the job by means of projects, networking with colleagues and outside professionals, expertise databases and peer review. It will become much more individuals' responsibility to ensure that they are up to date.

Formal development programmes will need to shift their focus and concentrate on providing individuals with the personal and leadership skills that will enable them to operate effectively in the New Organization. As I have already indicated, I believe that the nature of the organization will frequently run ahead of the ability of individuals to operate within it. A massive training and development effort will be needed to give more people the tools to survive and thrive. Coherent frameworks for such training for the future are scarce and so I will go into some detail in the next section to outline what I believe a core programme should include.

Building a network

In order to operate successfully in the boundaryless organization, most individuals need, literally, to develop a new mental map of how their organization functions. Many technical experts, for example, are relatively naive about the range of other resources available within their organizations, the political processes of influence required to mobilize such resources, the skills of gaining sponsorship and commitment to projects, the sensitive identification of client needs, the ongoing management of a client relationship and the ability to mobilize a disparate group of individuals through the stages of delivery of a know-how project to a client. They may also be quite naive about the nature of the different stakeholders within a client system and the politics of a client system. As Alan Kamman observes,

> the individuals in the organization must develop the skills required to participate in this information infrastructure. On the managerial level, this means developing the skills for motivating change amongst knowledge workers: on the knowledge worker level, this means the development of the skills that will bring their value added into the information infrastructure.[7]

Mapping networks

Where does the individual start. Kate Owen, the leader of the culture change team at BP, highlights three key elements of networking. 'The first is *having* a network, the second is *extending* your network and the third is *activating* your network.' Most people we find do not hold in their awareness the network that they already have. We do an exercise with them which is literally to ask them to draw themselves at the centre of their world. We call this 'Stakeholder Mapping'. We ask people to draw on a large sheet of paper all the key groups and individuals with whom they have contacts in order to get their work done. This includes people within their own organizations, within other organizations and institutions and also takes notice of the social and personal support systems and leisure elements that are a very important part of an individual's job success.

Figure 4.2 provides a check-list to help individuals identify all those people who may have either expectations of them in their role or contributions to make to their success. It also helps them become aware of the range of resources

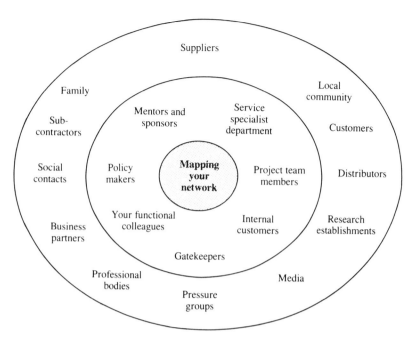

Figure 4.2 Mapping networks. © Colin Hastings, New Organisation Consulting. (This diagram may be reproduced freely with due acknowledgement.)

available to them to help them. They become aware, too, of how this direct network is, in turn, a gateway to other 'invisible' network members. When they see their charts compared with those of other colleagues, some of the gaps in their network become very evident. During this exercise they often identify some relationships where, perhaps, they have not invested sufficient time. Likewise, they often find that they have a bias in the way they use their time, making connections with people they feel comfortable with rather than those who are important.

Developing networking skills

The reality of organizational networking is that it is frequently difficult to get things done, that it makes considerable demands on individuals, that it requires balancing constant trade-offs and contradictions, that it creates stress, that it is riddled with conflict above the norm and that it requires individuals to embrace complexity and see the whole picture.[8] In short, it stretches individuals' capabilities to the limit. It is a very advanced form of organizing that needs very advanced kinds of people with very advanced skills. Both Digital and Gore, for example, have recognized this, particularly with new people coming into the organization, and have institutionalized development support in their idea of the personal mentor or sponsor. This is one effective mechanism for helping people to learn these skills rapidly, particularly if they have come from a very dissimilar organization.

In addition, many of the Pathfinders are investing heavily in providing development programmes in these skills, resources for self-development and simple guides to successful networking. However everybody—managers, mentors, sponsors, coaches, management developers and trainers—need to have some kind of coherent concept of what these network survival and operating skills are, so as to provide a common language within the organization to describe effective behaviours. Digital calls their's 'Decspeak'.

A skills framework

Such a framework is illustrated in Figure 4.3. It has two main elements. The first describes three stages that individuals go through in developing and leveraging their networks. These stages I have described as:

1   knowing the network
2   developing your network
3   mobilizing a network.

The second element is the five core personal networking processes. These in turn I have described as:

1   crossing boundaries
2 . exchange and reciprocity
3   alliance-building and conflict management
4   communication skills
5   personal management.

Let me describe each of these components a little bit more.

Knowing the network

In order to know the available resources and people within the network, individuals have to be aware of their organization, its structure, its business, its systems and its activities. They also have to be aware of the external linkages that the organization has. This requires of them a degree of open-mindedness, interest and curiosity to find out who is who, to identify some of the key people who are gatekeepers or access routes to the relevant information. It also requires that they either find out or that the organization provides the necessary information to be able to access such people.

Developing your network

Many people develop their network by means of the tasks that they undertake

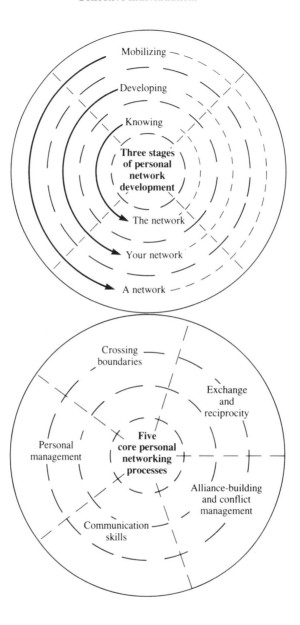

Figure 4.3 A framework for development of personal networking skills. © Colin Hastings, New Organisation Consulting. (This diagram may be reproduced freely with due acknowledgement.)

and, in so doing, extend it, not only through the people they work with, but the networks that these other individuals provide access to. Individuals need constantly to be thinking about ways in which they extend their networks and initiate contacts with people who could be useful to them in their jobs. They also need to be aware that even their current connections need to be sustained and maintained because networks die over time if they are not renewed in some way or other. This maintenance activity is an essential part of building quality, trusting relationships such that when they need to be mobilized this can be done quickly.

Mobilizing a network

This third stage is actually using other people to make things happen. It will involve cashing in the benefits of the first two stages, during which you have identified the people who have got what you want and those who need what you have. It will involve advocacy, making the case and providing leadership to encourage people and persuade them to follow the particular course of action required. It will also be about negotiating different kinds of both tangible and intangible resources from people. It might be, for example, negotiating for their time or money, people and materials. Alternatively, it may be more about securing their support for a particular project or their advice about the most appropriate timing for initiating something.

Crossing boundaries

People working in the New Organization will have to be very aware of the nature of different kinds of boundaries and, in particular, aware of their own reactions to such boundaries. They may not only have to cross physical boundaries (in the sense of different locations or countries), but they will encounter also political boundaries within the organization, psychological boundaries, mental boundaries and limitations, status boundaries, functional boundaries and even historical boundaries. All of these need to be understood and strategies developed for moving across them with fluency and ease where necessary.

Exchange and reciprocity

This core grouping of skills and qualities is to do with individuals' understanding the process of cooperation. They will have to understand how they can trade with other people within the network, how they can build up credits and, subsequently, cash them in and how they can exchange different currencies of different values to different people.

Alliance-building and conflict management

Much of the work of the New Organization will happen by means of alliances or a critical mass of people making the case and getting agreement to go forwards. This requires the ability to create a sense of common vision among people, negotiate and resolve conflicts concerning different objectives and means of achieving objectives and collective problem solving in order to find ways of meeting different objectives simultaneously. Understanding and managing conflicts on a continuous basis but within a collaborative framework and set of norms about joint problem solving and alliance formation will be very important.

Communication skills

Organizational networking will require a very wide range of both conventional and new communication skills of people. Clearly the normal repertoire of verbal and written skills will be required. Equally, the necessary skills for running meetings will need to be developed. However, in addition, people will need to be skilled at using the telephone and eventually will probably learn skills like video-conferencing effectively. In addition, it goes without saying that most individuals will need keyboard and software skills. We can also think of the skills of being a broker, passing on information and linking people together as being another aspect of communication skills.

Personal management

Organizational networking will produce many conflicts of demand and priority. The result, if not well-managed, will be overload and stress. Individuals will have to learn the skills of protecting their boundaries to some extent and of saying 'no'. They will also need to understand their own reactions to and strategies for coping with stress that will be an inevitable component of New Organization life.

4   Rewarding organizational networking

The rewards for the organization of getting the New Organization right will be that individuals stay and that the organization retains valuable know-how and contribution. Individuals, despite the stresses of working in such environments, will judge that, on balance, the rewards to them are worth the demands because their motivational needs are broadly met.

To get the reward equation right, though, some *new* answers are going to be required. On compensation and benefits, cooperative individualists will want the maximum flexibility and choice in their package. If your current system is highly stratified by rigid grades and tight rules about who can have what kind of benefit, then it is time to start taking the rewards edifice apart. Break down the ranges of benefits you offer and let people choose their mix of benefits up to a value that represents their contribution, their experience and their growing asset value to the organization. The so-called basket of benefits is not too difficult to achieve.

Rewarding know-how

Putting a value on people's contribution and asset value seems well nigh impossible at the moment, but nothing, of course, is impossible. There is an interesting network of business people, accountants, social scientists and academics working under the banner of a research institution called Neurope Lab, near Geneva, who are looking for answers to just such problems. What seems impossible now, will I believe become commonplace in the next decade.[9] So watch out for development in such areas as knowledge-based pay systems, knowledge auditing, knowledge asset valuation, knowledge-performance indicators and similar-sounding key words—theory about to become practice.

Peer ratings

One approach to reward and performance that is entirely consistent with New Organization principles is that people's performance should be rated by those they deal with most frequently. In a soft technology organization, this is complicated to organize, although peer assessment (performance evaluation by colleagues) is beginning to be used. However, once hard networking technologies are fully installed inside and outside the organization, a whole new set of possibilities open up for individuals to measure and be measured and receive performance feedback from all those they service, both inside and outside the organization. Where Pathfinders such as ABB, WHO The Healthy Cities Project and DPE make the performance of units transparent to all, there can be no reason in principle why eventually the performance of individuals throughout a network cannot be compared and made visible electronically.

The new status symbols

As for non-financial rewards, the very concept of the New Organization is based on the premise of trying to design in motivators to the very fabric and processes of the organization itself. This will mean major changes to the traditional motivators of status and recognition. In these flatter and more flexible models, status and recognition will have to come in different currencies. Your status in this kind of organization will derive from your connections, from the degree to which you are seen to help others to get their jobs done and to help them to find the resources and information they require. Your status will come from your ability to collaborate. Your status will also be recognized not by the *depth* of your knowledge, necessarily, but by the *breadth* of your knowledge (see Box 4.1 for ways in which to give people recognition). Charles Handy,[10] the British management writer, refers to this as the horizontal fast track, by means of which the individual is valued for a growing portfolio of marketable skills and, being

Box 4.1   How to give people recognition

- Ask them to undertake special projects that are important to the organization.
- Invite outside visitors to come in and hear about their work.
- Ask them for advice or for contacts.
- Publicize their achievements inside and outside the organization.
- Defend or express confidence in them in a public situation.
- Ask them to represent the company at a conference, professional or industry body or in the local community.
- Have them pass on their skills and experience to others.
- Spot opportunities that interest them that they would not be aware of.
- Assign them resources.

increasingly able to appreciate the big picture with all its complicated trade-offs and interactions.

Recognition of individuals will also, increasingly, need to take many forms. As in the Danish Biotechnology case, a fundamental means of recognition will be that of giving people autonomy, trusting them to make judgements about what is in the best interests of the organization and coaching or mentoring them to accelerate their ability to do this. Charles Handy also advocates wider use of the power of the by-line in journalism, that is the person's name on the article is a most potent form of recognition and autonomy. Yet, in how many organizations do reports by 'subordinates' still go forward with the boss's name on them where they have indeed been authored by more junior people. Gifford Pinchot, author of *Intrapreneuring*[11] points out, too, that being given resources to pursue one's particular interests is a potent form of recognition and a symbol of trust that organizations could well use more extensively.

Understanding what makes the new and scarce knowledge workers tick and thinking radically and strategically about how to help them to operate effectively is one of the main drivers behind interest in New Organization concepts. It is these individuals who are the key assets and building blocks of the New Organization and in response to whose changing demands and needs the Organizational Networking culture needs to be grown.

References

1 Kreiner, Kristian and Majken Schultz (1990) 'Crossing the Institutional Divide ... Networking in Biotechnology', EUREKA Managment Research Initiative, Copenhagen Business School.

2 Maccoby, Michael (1988) *Why Work?*, Simon and Schuster, New York.
3 Maccoby, Michael (1988) ibid.
4 Moss Kanter, Rosabeth (1983) *The Change Masters*, George Allen and Unwin, London.
5 Barham, Kevin (1991) 'Networking—the corporate way round international discord', *Multinational Business*, No. 4, 1990/91, pp 1–11.
6 Maccoby, Michael (1991) ibid.
7 Kamman, Alan *Global Networks, Stage by Stage*, Nolan Norton & Co. Lexington, Masschusetts.
8 Gasser, Thomas (1991) *Managing Without Boundaries: the challenge to business*, European Forum for Management Development, Brussels, pp 8–11.
9 Neurope Lab (1991) Proceedings of Forum on Knowledge as an asset, November, Archamps, France.
10 Handy, Charles (1991) 'Reflections on the Future', presentation to Association of Management Education and Development Conference, The 21st Century Organisation, June, London.
11 Pinchot, Gifford (1985) *Intrapreneuring*, Harper & Row, New York.

Textiles

Try wandering around the fabric department of a large store. Wander not only into the dressmaking fabrics section, but also into the household furnishings fabrics section. You may even stray into the carpets section. What all these materials have in common is a warp and a weft. These are the horizontal and vertical strands of yarn that are interwoven to give the fabric its strength and pliability. The image so far is a bit too much like the conventional hierarchical and functionally divided organization, the vertical and the lateral you may think. Well, perhaps our New Organization will still have these simple elements at its heart.

Look more closely, though. Observe the tremendous range of yarns that are used; the design and pattern that is printed on the surface of the material or woven in with multicoloured yarn; the fact that some materials do not have flat surfaces, but have bumpy or rough surfaces; the fact that for many materials you cannot even see the structure of the warp and the weft but, instead, you see a kaleidoscope of colour and texture. Take your thinking one step further and, instead of laying the material out flat, fold it over. Fold it over again and again and back on itself. Crunch it up into a ball. Cut it. Assemble it in different ways, sew it together, make a curtain out of it in two dimensions. Make a garment out of it in three dimensions or more. Make a patchwork quilt out of it. Make an organization out of it.

5
Soft networking—how to keep the feeling of being small as we grow bigger

PATHFINDER
World Health Organization: The Healthy Cities Project

The project concept

In the early 1980s, the World Health Organization evolved the strategy of 'Health for All'. In the process of trying to give this strategy some teeth and to find effective ways of implementing it, the WHO regional office for Europe evolved 'The Healthy Cities Project' during 1985.

The vision behind the Healthy Cities Project was that of targeting a group of volunteer cities that would experiment with new ways of promoting health and improving the environment. The focus would be on stimulating action for promoting health at city level. The purpose was also to change people's view of health as a purely medical matter to one of more general importance, that it had to be high on the agenda of political decision makers, key groups in the city and the population at large. A further fundamental part of its philosophy was to recognize that, in order to succeed in its goals, the Healthy Cities Project had to make prevention and health promotion a highly visible enterprise supported by the community. This philosophy was neatly encapsulated in the Healthy Cities Project Mission and Purpose Statement, which is, 'to build a new public health movement in the cities of Europe and to make health *everyone's* business at the city level'. As Ilona Kickbusch, who initiated the WHO Healthy Cities Project, put it, 'the simple idea was to help people who live in cities work on the simple question "how do we make our cities better places to live in?"'

The guiding values

Those cities that became members of the project were joining a network that was guided and given purpose and direction by a strong set of organizing principles. They were joining or expressing their commitment to a product in the form of 11 measurable qualities of a healthy city, which defined the goals or performance standards towards which they agreed to work. What they also committed to was a broad process for achieving these ends.

The nature of this process is founded on some very clear values. The first is a strong belief in both the power of and the need to recognize diversity. 'Diversity was a key idea from the start . . . the cities form a pluralistic group with different political systems and ideologies. . . . This diversity is essential if we are willing to embark on natural experiments and social innovations that attempt to open new avenues.'[1]

A second core element of the process was the belief in cooperative strategies.

> Cooperative strategies . . . recognize that the major conflicts facing humanity can only be solved through joint efforts rather than confrontational strategies. Clearly, efforts to break the deadlock in many areas of health policy, particularly in the financing and provision of care, could profit from new views and strategies . . . political negotiation and consensus building at city level become a key strategy to move the project forward.[2]

Such a philosophy also had implications for the role of WHO in the project. How was it to exercise its 'managerial' role? Its power base was seen as one that enabled rather than directed, which mobilized 'power to' rather than 'power over'.

Another important element at this early stage was a strong branding of the product. From the earliest stages, its logo has been promulgated throughout the cities and throughout its publications. An active approach to the use of the media has also characterized the project at all levels. The logo provides a positive identity for the project. Its design, however, is also cunning in that it enables each city to interpret the logo according to its local situation, while the logo remains instantly identifiable right across the project cities (see Figure 5.1).

The criteria for joining

The fundamental criterion for being designated a project city was that there should be clear political commitment within the city to the objectives and the process of the project. In practice, this meant that the cities had to offer evidence of being able to either offer or be prepared to put in place rapidly, the following elements:

1   they had to be prepared to formulate and implement health promotion plans

that involved all the different sectors within a city, such as housing, transport, leisure, medical, industrial and educational
2   they had to secure the necessary resources to pursue and implement the plan
3   they had to be prepared to report back regularly on progress to WHO and to share information and experience from their practice with other project cities and partners
4   they had to be prepared to support the development of a national network of healthy cities within their own country
5   they had to establish an intersectoral political steering committee to act as a focus for and to steer the project, which, in practice, would often involve people in areas such as housing, transport, leisure facilities, health and environmental health services all working together, very often for the first time
6   they had to establish a project office with a full-time project leader and resources
7   they had to be prepared to create mechanisms for public participation in public health issues, particularly via work with the media
8   they had to carry out population health surveys designed to measure the achievement against Healthy City goals
9   they were expected to develop a local network of research institutions and other interested bodies to support the activities of the project
10 they were expected to develop active working links with other project cities, fostering both technical and cultural exchange and be prepared to host Healthy Cities meetings and events within their city.

Such a demanding set of criteria filtered out a large number of applications. In early 1986, the first 11 cities were designated and joined the project. In early 1988 an additional 14 joined and since then a further 10 cities joined. These 35 cities form the elements of the Healthy City Project and the 'nodes' of diverse networks that are so vital to its success.

The local city network

Activity at the local city level is coordinated by the project office whose job is to forge a large number of alliances among partners in the pursuit of the overall mission and purpose. This might involve, for example, partnership among very diverse institutions and groupings, such as the departments of a local city's administration, local industry and business, local district administrations within a city, local voluntary organizations, local and national media, housing organizations, consumer groups, ethnic organizations, universities and other research institutions. The role of the project office is to support and enable, to devolve power to these groupings to promote initiatives, but within the very clear objectives, framework and philosophies.

Figure 5.1 Branding a network: the WHO Healthy Cities Project.

National networks

The strong entry criteria for designated cities were designed to create robust, successful models and examples for others. The forum for other interested cities within a country was created using the mechanism of the national networks. WHO assisted in setting up national network offices whose job was to stimulate interest among other cities within the country, using the designated project cities as model catalysts. Not all the cities linked by means of national networks work strictly to the requirements of the WHO project cities, but they are agreeing to work in this general direction.

Intercity collaboration

The sharing of learning and ideas among the target project cities lies at the heart of the process that enables the ideals and practical applications of the project's ideology become more widely disseminated. By means of an intense process of recording and transmitting this learning, problems, pitfalls and success stories are rapidly transmitted. This process is partially orchestrated by the role of WHO Europe. In addition, cities are encouraged to make direct links with each other either in regional groupings based on language or through joint projects. WHO has formalized such collaboration around specific themes of particular interest to small groups of cities who cooperate to formulate a 'Multi-city Action Plan' (MCAP). One very successful MCAP concerning the subject of AIDS strategies involves experts from Liverpool, Rotterdam, Seville and Gothenburg working as a project team to examine and improve each others' AIDS strategies in conjunction with technical experts from WHO itself. 'For these MCAPs to work effectively', said Lisbeth Shore, the WHO AIDS programme coordinator, 'it's important that people don't stand on professional dignity—they have to be prepared to share not only the successes but also the failures.' Other MCAPs are at various stages of development on themes such as smoking, health-promoting hospitals and the specific needs of the Baltic states.

External networks

Another grouping within the network, which has been explicitly fostered by the project, is the joining together of external resources that can provide services to any part of the project. Some university departments and research establishments in particular have become heavily identified with the project. In addition, the project has utilized external contractors and consultants to carry out some of the internal research and monitoring processes as well as to develop training and publications. At a higher level, WHO has initiated moves to collaborate with other partners. They have, for example, embarked on related joint activities with the Council of Europe. This and other initiatives, such as joint work with the

Commission of the European Community, the Organization for Economic Co-operation and Development and the United Nations Economic Commission for Europe, are all part of a concerted strategy to gain political commitment to the principles underlying the project.

Learning and support mechanisms

While the mission, the goals, the guiding values and the criteria for joining provide for a strong sense of direction, much more has been provided to ensure the cooperative processes upon which the project is founded. A very wide range of mechanisms for communication and sharing of information have been put in place that serve to exchange learning, provide support and to hold the overall project together while simultaneously enabling a wide range of diverse initiatives. This has become known as the Information Exchange and Consultation Strategy. It was designed to act as a continuous monitor of the process of the project itself so that its own internal ways of working could continuously be reviewed in the light of experience. The objectives of the plan were four-fold:

1 to highlight key issues within the overall project
2 to identify resources within the network and make these available on a more widespread basis
3 to identify and disseminate models of good practice
4 to provide expert consultation to the cities on aspects of both technical and policy provision.

Much work has also been put into developing indicators of performance for the main health targets being measured by the project and assistance is given to cities both in measuring and surveying these and adapting them to their local circumstances. These measures are taken at designated intervals and communicated widely across cities in a transparent fashion, providing both information and a certain sense of competition and opportunity for comparison between cities.

To complement these measurement and analytical processes, there has been a heavy investment in a range of communication mechanisms. Each year there have been two major 'business meetings'. These bring together the project leaders and key members of the project teams from different cities and take part in different cities within the network each year. They are strongly focused on technical issues and exchanging experience. Once a year, in addition, there are larger conferences and symposiums where a much wider range of people attend, drawing in not only those directly involved in the projects, but the wider network of politicians and other vested interests within the cities who have an important role to play. In parallel with these formal conferences, there is a growing programme of workshops, training courses and other *ad hoc* meetings of taskforces addressing specific issues. One such workshop, for example, grew out of an initiative by the city of Nancy in France on the topic of health indicators.

Other workshops have taken place to provide training in project leadership skills for project leaders who frequently do not have these management skills.

The project has also developed a very active PR and publications policy. Some have emanated from WHO itself in the form of a series of Healthy Cities papers. Elsewhere in the network, a newsletter—*Positive Health*—is published by WHO in association with a major health promotion organization in Wales. Short leaflets have been produced (sponsored by commercial organizations) and other initiatives have been taken within the network. A major evaluation report has also been produced after two years and a further one is planned at the five-year point.[3] Such reports are widely disseminated both within and beyond the healthy cities movement and distil the experience of the cities by means of analysis of detailed questionnaires and interviews. There are also a growing range of training materials evolving that are often being developed in one city and then made available to others. A booklet entitled 'Twenty Steps for Developing a Healthy Cities Project'[4] has been produced that summarizes the key activities in starting up a successful Healthy Cities Project. This booklet will now be disseminated widely to all other cities wishing to start up similar programmes, even if they are not officially part of the designated Healthy Cities Project, and will be used as the basis for training of new project leaders and their teams. Although the working language of the project is English, the two-year review report was translated into German, Spanish, Greek, French and Japanese and the 'Twenty Steps' is being made available in most European languages.

These research reports have been written up and fed back to the individual cities. Also the lessons learned have been aggregated and the results made available to all the cities. In addition, a computerized database is being developed of all initiatives and key contacts within the cities. This computerized database will be able to be accessed by all participating cities and national networks. Alongside this, a multilingual Healthy Cities Project bibliography is being developed on specialist topics.

A taste of success

There is a strong feeling within WHO that if the current number of 35 formal project cities is increased to any more than 40–45, it will become difficult to sustain. However, by creating a fluid group of networks at different levels, cutting across different boundaries, they would appear to have created a self-sustaining system that can overcome some of the potential limits on size.

It has undoubtedly provided an advanced model of how to structure and support several interrelated networks, creating both a free and open flow of information in all directions, while also using project planning and thinking techniques to focus and coordinate people's activity on results. In addition, its use of research, conferences, training and a wide range of media, together with the well-articulated role of WHO itself as an enabler of the network, have broken new ground and provided important models for others.

There are only two questions to ask . . . the first is 'Who has what I need?' and the second is 'Who needs what I have?'
Pauli Kulvik, Managing Director, Nest OY, Finland

1   Accelerating personal networks

While the hard technologies are all about linking computers, the soft technologies are all about mechanisms and processes for linking people. There is seldom a coherent strategy taken by organizations in deploying the full range of such tools available to them. That coherence tends to be reserved only for the hard technologies at least in theory. Organizations should and must intervene actively to orchestrate, initiate and accelerate the development of personal networks by means of coherent strategies for soft communications technologies. This chapter examines a number of ways in which this can be done.

Simply because most of the soft technologies are relatively commonplace, most managers do not make the connection between these different tools, all of which help to accelerate and extend the range of people's networks. Because many of the tools are familiar, and are, indeed, relatively traditional, insufficient innovation has been applied to the aim of getting the best out of them in an organizational setting.

Investing in soft technologies

You should be under no illusion, however, that these traditional technologies come cheap. While I have never seen any quantitative data that summarizes the scale of investment in such tools and activities, of one thing I am certain—the scale of investment is and has to be substantial. Surely companies ought to be thinking hard about how to get greater payback from this type of investment. After all, it is investment in the widening of personal networks throughout the organization that will become a key factor in enabling companies to preserve the innovative, responsive feeling of small organizations as they grow larger. It is investment in the ability of people who know each other within the corporation to make quick contact, know how each other is likely to think, assemble resources rapidly and make quick decisions based on having worked together before that will be the key to retaining the benefits of smallness. There are some who feel that electronic communications will supersede some of these more traditional person-to-person connection-type tools. I believe that this is nonsense. The evidence that emerges from the Pathfinders described in this book and other organizations suggests that companies should start with the building of personal social networks and that the communications technologies follow afterwards as a means of making already established connections easier to manage and to make. The person-to-person relationship is and will continue to be the fundamental building block of effectiveness in both current and new organizations. Communications technology alone cannot provide this.

Conferring

When I was running programmes at Ashridge Management College, I found repeatedly that, in common with most business schools, participants found one of the major values of the courses to be simply mixing with and talking to people from other parts of their own company or from other companies. However, people also said that there was 'not enough time set aside in the programme for this informal mixing'. 'It takes a certain quality of time', said one participant 'to really get to learn from other people's experience. And that's one of the most profound benefits of this kind of occasion.' I find the same issue comes up when I talk at large conferences. Conferences should be for 'conferring', but the sponsors of people coming to such conferences look for a programme packed full of formal activities. The more sessions crammed into a short space of time, the better 'value' the conference is perceived to offer.

There is a large number of ways in which people from different parts of organizations can be brought together to confer. These include the annual chairman's conference for senior management, the annual sales conference, the 'dealers' conference and various other types of meetings both formal and informal. Some organizations expend lavish amounts of money on prestigious locations, high-quality entertainment and glitz and sophisticated PR and media support. Increasingly, these occasions bring together international groupings, but a frequent criticism of them from participants is that they become set pieces, formal occasions in which the delegates are given a rousing talk by senior management, where they are loaded with large quantities of information by a series of speakers and where they go away, ostensibly, motivated by the experience to deliver the next year's targets. While this type of conferencing model may well achieve *some* benefit in motivation, it usually fails to link different people from the different parts of the organizations together so that relationships can be built. Very little attention is given to the design of the process at the conference to enable such relationship building to take place in other than a haphazard manner. There are usually 'social functions' built into the programme where this is supposed to happen and, indeed, it does, but frequently these occasions become the times when old friends get to see each other again and catch up rather than occasions where new relationships get forged.

Senior management should be demanding more tangible outputs and paybacks from such expensive investments of people's time. There is now an emerging set of meeting and conference design skills (involving structured mixing processes and careful design of conference tasks, groupings and outputs) that quite explicitly address the issue of how you can rapidly build large numbers of network relationships and linkages in a short space of time. These accelerated networking processes will, more and more, become significant features of large meetings and conferences in the future.

Inclusivity

Another way in which such conferences fall short of their potential is in the exclusivity of the groupings they tend to bring together. How many organizations hold conferences and seminars where they quite deliberately try to bring a very wide mix of roles, levels, countries and divisions together? How many companies hold international conferences only for people at management level, denying the opportunity for networking development to those at the operational level who, in many ways, would gain more day-to-day benefit from intraorganizational linkages? How many organizations mix together their suppliers, clients, shopfloor workers, research scientists, middle managers, external advisers, consultants and so on in the same setting? How many organizations try to create in these settings a visible microcosm of the wider, extended network that comprises the organization in the fullest sense? How many organizations really use these kinds of activities to break down boundaries and extend the membership of some of the exclusive clubs that so clearly dominate our organizational life? There is still, at many company conferences, a sense that an exclusive club is being brought together, that attendance at the conference is, in some way, a mark of status and privilege. These underlying, though frequently unstated attitudes, are quite inimicable to building networks.

Designing the process

It can be done, but great attention needs to be paid to the design of the process, the way in which the conference functions and groups of people interact. Conferences in the future will be better designed, orchestrated and, frequently, with these ambitious objectives, facilitated. The days of the extravagant, motivational conference are over. Conferences will become visible and living images of the total organization for short periods of time, doing *real* work in order to make rapid progress on issues that require the participation and involvement of large numbers of people.

In this sense, I see conferencing activity moving more towards the realm of management and organizational development. Companies such as British Airways, ABB and BP invest in workshops and related development activities designed to involve large numbers of people in realizing change. They realize the power of such activities when they are properly resourced, designed and conducted. Other companies, such as Olivetti with its 'no frontiers' management programme[5] and Electrolux with its international managers' programme, recognize that management development and training courses are another powerful tool through which these cross-boundary relationships can be developed. Such companies are using these devices to turn outsiders into insiders.

Conversely, how many companies actively encourage their people to go out to external conferences with the explicit objective of cultivating networks and access to information and expertise. Once again, this kind of activity is often a perk or a reward for the senior expert in a particular area. Why not open out the whole concept and see the moving of your people into the outside world as part of your organization's search for the very best of expertise, the very best of market information, the very best of exposing your people to the realities faced by clients, suppliers and communities.

One small word of warning, however. Managers in one company recently talked to me about 'workshop fatigue' where people become involved in so many conferencing-type activities that they simply cannot cope with any more. Even if, 'real work' is being done in this medium, it is quite demanding and exhausting. People need time to recuperate and work solo to complement this type of activity.

Mobility policies

In the oil and construction industries, it has, for some years, been quite common practice that a team from the client company be located within the offices of the subcontractors or vice versa. This is an attempt to make closer connections, to create a single unit from diverse parties or partners and thus foster more effective team working. IBM has, for some considerable time, created joint programmes between its business divisions, research and development laboratories and related university departments. However, James McGroddy, the Director of IBM's research laboratory at Yorktown Heights, 35 miles north of New York, has gone way beyond this. He has promoted a policy of what he calls 'entanglement'. 'It involves sending research fellows to other parts of IBM and getting people from other parts of IBM to work at research. People work together better if they know each other', he reasons.[6] He also finds the mechanism highly effective in the race to get things onto the market more quickly, 'like strawberries before they rot'. Speeding products to the market-place has been made easier by this rich interchange and infrastructure.

Entanglement

International and cross-unit postings, mobility and job rotation of this nature are now well-proven mechanisms that help link people and extend their understanding of the conditions and opportunities beyond their own part of the organization.

ABB, for example, invests heavily in this kind of system. Such mobility policies help to build understanding between units and also between the centre of the corporation and its units. As people move, they not only take with them access to their own network, but their know-how of the other parts of the organization, which they can, in turn, invest in the new situation. They learn how to talk the language of different organizational groupings (not only the national language but the cultural and technical languages). The networks that evolve in this manner will be particularly cohesive among people who share the binding experience of a common work history, especially where this has involved cooperative victories and the accomplishment of difficult tasks. The benefit that comes from being comrades in adversity is a very special kind of togetherness.

Box 5.1   The tandem career

Dual-career couples have particular problems when one partner is offered a job in another country. In a company like Shell, foreign experience is vital to management progression. Huub Donkers from Shell Chemicals in Rotterdam faced just such a problem when he was offered a post in the UK because his wife, Marese, was also employed by Shell as a technologist.

Shell, however, came up with a creative solution. They call it the tandem career, where the company does all it can to plan their separate careers together. IBM Europe also tries to do the same. 'The company realizes we are a package deal', said a couple about to relocate from the UK to Paris.

Beyond the jobs themselves, more and more companies are offering widespread help with house-hunting, finding schooling for children and language and cultural awareness training in order to cut down on the stress and disruption to family life involved in moving countries. Getting it right creates happy and productive employees; getting it wrong is very expensive.

Summarized from *The Independent*, page 23, 10 May, 1991,

London.

One company that has particularly shown the way is the international telecommunications company Ericsson. It has invested a great deal in 'people linking processes', which employ such devices as temporary assignments and joint teams. What makes Ericsson perhaps stand out is its long-standing policy of transferring large numbers of people back and forth between its headquarters and subsidiaries. Christopher Bartlett and Sumantra Ghoshal of the Harvard Business School compare this with the more parsimonious approach taken by Ericsson's competitor NEC.

Where NEC may transfer a new technology through a few key managers,

Ericsson will send a team of 50 or 100 engineers and managers from one unit to another for a year or two; while NEC's flow is primarily from headquarters to subsidiary, Ericsson's is a balanced two-way flow with people coming to the parent not only to learn but also to bring their expertise; and while NEC's transfers are predominantly Japanese, Ericsson's multidirectional process involves all nationalities.

Australian technicians seconded to Stockholm in the mid 1970s to bring their experience with digital switching into the corporate development effort established enduring relationships that helped in the subsequent joint development of a rural switch in Australia a decade later. Confidences built when a 40-man Italian team spent 18 months in Sweden in the early 1970s to learn about electronic switching, provided the basis for the subsequent decentralization of software development and the delegation of responsibility for developing the corporate transmission systems to the Italian company.[7]

We can see here a stunning level of commitment to mobility and interunit 'entanglement' very much at the operational level.

Lateral promotions

Another mechanism that fosters such mobility is the organization's attitude to career development. Digital has abandoned the notion of career development because of its implicit assumptions to do with climbing a ladder of status and hierarchy. Instead, they have substituted the idea of personal development paths. Individuals develop their working experience by means of a sequence of moves into and out of different parts of the organization. This develops both networks and a broader understanding of the overall business.

Becton Dickinson, the US medical electronics company, has been working out similar approaches. As Brian Dumaine of *Fortune*, the American magazine observes,

It's likely that tomorrow's workers and managers, instead of slowly climbing the ladder, will make more lateral moves, picking up expertise in different functions like marketing or manufacturing. ... Becton Dickinson is trying out so-called lateral promotions, rotating, say, a financial person into a marketing or manufacturing job. In one division last year, the company rotated 10 managers out of 50. These people got a raise and change of title, just as they would with a regular promotion, but they weren't necessarily put in charge of any more people.[8]

Building design

From the 1960s right through to the 1980s, corporate architecture has been dominated by that symbol of status and hierarchy—the skyscraper. Rationalized as a response to soaring land values in city centre sites, the skyscraper became a manifestation of opulence and truly a physical expression of the dominant hierarchical, bureaucratic model of organization. Its many-layered structure, broken into regularly shaped vertical and lateral boxes and squares, with the senior management offices and dining rooms always on the top floors was patently obvious to everyone for what it was: a picture in physical form of the hierarchical organization that the managers within held in their heads. We are living now with the practical and damaging results of these fantasies.

Mark Alpert,[9] writing in *Fortune*, wryly observes that the Americans have had to create the whole new specialization—'organizational ecologists'—to come up with the not very startling finding that the frequency of face-to-face communication among employees falls off sharply if they are separated by more than two floors. Those of us who have worked in these corporate monstrosities have for years been aware of this fact and seen its consequences. Such buildings are disastrous for organizational networking.

However, thankfully, some new and exciting thinking is beginning to emerge. If you go into Digital's main building outside Reading, to the west of London, you walk down a long, straight, open area known as 'the street'. Overhead the flags of many nations hang symbolically. To the side, a bank, a shop, large indoor plants and small circular tables and chairs create the atmosphere of a sidewalk café. The street is where people meet.

If you go to the headquarters of Norsk Data in Scandinavia, you enter an architectural world that more resembles in feel and style a busy market-place or university campus. There are comfortable seating areas, tastefully decorated, as any person might expect their home to be, with pictures, plants and comfortable furniture. In all the nooks and crannies there are people in huddles talking and working together. There are open spaces in which people criss-cross continuously, bumping into each other, holding short conversations and moving on again. The whole building sprawls over a wide area and its different parts are easy to get to.

Åke Larson, the Swedish architect who designed the Norsk Data building, also designed a building called The Ark, which rises like an ocean liner alongside the Hammersmith flyover in London. Figure 5.2 shows something of the atmosphere created within. The following extract from the information pack about it describes its design philosophy.

> The Ark . . . is created around an idea. The same idea that organic companies are created around. Those companies we call 'third wave companies'. . . . They see it as a living organism: and what gives it life are the humans in it, and their ability to seek, find and utilize information.
>
> The Ark is created round this concept. Like the Ark of Noah, it is an escape. An escape from obsolete values. An escape from obsolete forms of organization. An escape from the traditional, centrally governed business into a network-oriented one. . . . An open concept, designed for people to communicate, to help ideas flow, to make information come alive. You might even say, to give chance

The small square outside
the auditorium.

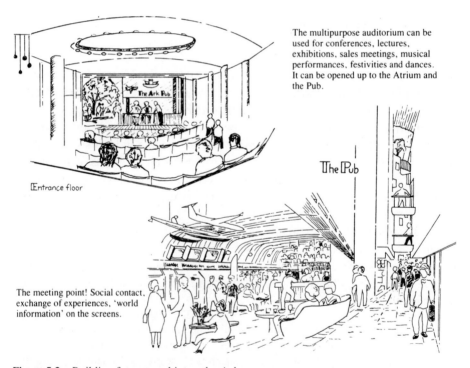

The multipurpose auditorium can be
used for conferences, lectures,
exhibitions, sales meetings, musical
performances, festivities and dances.
It can be opened up to the Atrium and
the Pub.

Entrance floor

The Pub

The meeting point! Social contact,
exchange of experiences, 'world
information' on the screens.

Figure 5.2   Building for networking—the Ark.

a chance. The Ark is designed to make it easy for people to meet, to relax, to
discuss, to exchange ideas . . . a town under a roof.

The same feeling of buzz and interaction lies behind three buildings described by

Mark Alpert. New out-of-town headquarters buildings for Nike outside Portland, Oregon, for Becton Dickinson in Franklin Lakes, New Jersey and for Trinova in Maumee, an outer suburb of Toledo, all bear testament to a growing awareness of the importance of architectural design on the way that an organization actually functions. He observes that, 'instead of making grand statements about corporate identity, these new buildings will be designed to perform productivity enhancing functions like encouraging communication among employees. . . . To maximize communication, architects are designing low-rise office buildings with numerous break areas, concourses and atriums where employees can meet and mingle casually.' The headquarters of Rhône-Poulenc & Rorer, 30 miles north west of Philadelphia, has five main buildings arranged in a semi-circle

> 'and connected by a curved three-storey 'circulation spine' that stands in front of them. This layout will compel employees to walk down the spine to reach common amenities such as the cafeteria and the fitness center. The notion is that a chance encounter between a chemist and a marketing manager, or a biologist and a regulatory expert, could germinate an idea or speed development of a new drug. . . .' says Robert Cawthorn, now CEO of the merged company: 'we wanted to put the R&D people next to the marketing and business people. We wanted to encourage interaction, because that's where all the good ideas come from'.[10]

Buildings have to accommodate and complement the new pictures of organization that are beginning to emerge. They must bring people together in different groupings and in different places in circumstances that are conducive to effective interaction, the exchange of ideas and high-performance team working. The whole fabric, technological infrastructure and support services have to be designed around this networking process. So, we should not be surprised to see 'offices' becoming more like university campuses or the stimulating café or market society of a thriving town. Neither should we be surprised to see offices becoming more like homes or communities in their style and ethos, places that people will actually want to go to work in because of the stimulation and the fun that they provide.

Conventional technologies

There is a strong case to be made for investing in conventional technologies such as travel, telephones, faxes and the printed word as the most important network-ing tools in the modern world. Those who dream of replacing air travel and the printed word with electronic communications will disagree. The fundamental element of these simple technologies, as compared with the advanced technolo-gies, is in their technological simplicity. One of the delights of the telephone and the fax is that their 'technologicalness' is relatively invisible. It does not intrude into the individual's experience in the same way that the 'technologicalness' of E-mail or videoconferencing does. It is this degree of perceived intrusion and complexity that is the major factor when users talk about user-friendliness. No organization should ignore the major contributions to networking that can be achieved by investing more systematically in simple technologies before being seduced by the promises of the advanced technologies. Some of the simpler soft technologies in suitable combinations may, at least in the initial phases of building the New Organization, provide quicker and easier pay-offs.

Telephone and fax

Contrary to what many people believe, the fax is an old-fashioned technology. That is one of the reasons for its being a very friendly technology. No sophisticated knowledge of keyboards, modems or networking protocols, file transfers or other such jargon is required. Most people find it easy to just tap out a telephone number on the keys and send through either a handwritten or typed document or, even more advantageous, pictures or diagrams. The fax has, almost unnoticed, revolutionized person-to-person communication between locations, both within countries and across the world. As the features available expand, it is able to do, although admittedly on a smaller scale, some of the things that E-mail can do. It can send the same document to a number of different people, although not necessarily simultaneously. It can dial in to other people's faxes and take back from them messages that have been left on it in advance. It can send automatically overnight so that documents and drawings are waiting as people arrive at their offices the next morning or as they work on the other side of the globe at the same time.

Another delightful feature of the fax, and I'm not sure how this norm has arisen, is that although in most business situations handwritten letters are unacceptable, it is entirely acceptable to send a handwritten note on the fax. It has acquired a degree of acceptable informality about it that is entirely appropriate to the culture of the New Organization.

Likewise, the telephone is undergoing a new lease of life as more and more sophisticated services have developed on the back of the new international and local digital networks. While its technologicalness is in danger of increasing too much (most users of digital telephones with sophisticated features only use, regularly, about a tenth of the available features and do not know how to operate the others), nevertheless, even in its simplest push-button form, it still remains a miracle of technology (albeit one that we take for granted). To be able to pick up a telephone in London and, within seconds, be talking to someone in New York, Tokyo, Johannesburg or Rome still amazes. Yet, a survey by British Telecom International demonstrated that at least half of managers are still afraid or inhibited about making international calls even though it is now so easy to do so. There is clearly plenty of scope, yet, for development in this technology. People build relationships on the telephone as, indeed, they are now beginning to do through the fax.

Telephone conferencing

One surprisingly underutilized facility is the concept of the telephone conference. The idea here is that people in different locations can all be connected together on the telephone simultaneously so that they can, in effect, hold a meeting on the telephone. The utilization of such services and their penetration of the market is still extremely low.

Here is a very cheap technology that really can make a difference. One of its intriguing characteristics is that it forces people to prepare better in advance for meetings. It also requires that the meeting be well structured and well run if it is not to degenerate into chaos. There is something about the fact that people are aware of the cost of the conference that also makes them think more about how best to use the time in a way that seldom happens when people meet together face-to-face in the same room. The costs are, in fact, minimal, certainly compared with the costs of people travelling to the same location.

Voice mail

Another unnoticed revolution related to the telephone system was the invention of the answer machine and its more up-to-date cousin voice mail. Although detested by many, these little robots have, once again, revolutionized the way that people work. They have enabled a whole generation of people who work from home to be able to service clients very satisfactorily. Likewise, they assist communication and networking greatly by relieving some of the frustration of telephoning and finding people are not available (so-called telephone tag), thus enabling people to make contact at mutually beneficial times.

Given the relatively low cost and the ease of use of modern telephone and fax communications, it behoves all organizations to think very seriously about investing in these technologies as a crucial way of building networks and interconnections both inside and outside the company. There will certainly be some situations, as we have seen already, where organizations can achieve *all* their objectives using *only* these simple technologies. They should also be studying seriously how to achieve better returns on their current investments in these technologies and see them as key tools for building and extending their organizational networking.

Travel

A theme running right through many of the Pathfinders examples is that of travel and the personal contacts that arise from it. ABB, Benetton, WHO (World Health Organization) and DPE all stress the importance of not only meeting colleagues, counterparts and customers around the world, but also experiencing their different situations and cultures at first hand. While there are many who thought that the IT revolution would kill off business travel, most of the airlines, at least, appear to strongly believe that the market will expand in the foreseeable future, despite its expense.

Study tours

One specific form of travel is much underutilized and that is the idea of the study tour. Japanese industrialists have for years been avid travellers abroad, not just in their stereotypical role as avid photographers of tourist sites. They are even more avid about their observing and learning as they tour the plants of other companies. This, perhaps is industrial espionage with a respectable face or let us just call it a hunger for learning. Certainly in the UK motor industry and at the Rover Group in particular (as with General Motors in the USA), some of the formative events in their turnaround of industrial relations resulted from exposing their shopfloor workers to the Japanese motor industry by means of a series of visits by shop stewards and shopfloor groups. Real attention needs to be paid to such events to ensure that these are active learning experiences and not just 'boondoggles' (USA), 'jollies' (UK) or passive sightseeing.

Another in-company variant of the study tour is used by Kodak. They send groups of people to different plants world-wide to make benchmarking visits or 'quality audits'. The idea here is that people from different plants will observe and measure the performance of other plants, rather as external consultants might, and will make recommendations about ways in which things could be improved. As Brian Pettet, an experienced production manager said, 'whilst it is easy from the outside to tell the others what they need to do to improve, if I am honest I always come back with more ideas about how my own plant can be improved. It's a very salutary experience to have to audit someone else's performance'.

These visits build up important cross-unit relationships as groups from the different locations work together on real problems. They create tasks and mechanisms that enable people to interact and work together directly at operational levels. This grass roots networking I am convinced is one way in which companies can achieve immediate tangible benefits from interlinkages.

Simple media

The printed word plays an important role in many of the Pathfinders' and other networking organizations. Paper-based media are something that we now take so much for granted that perhaps, again, we fail to examine creative ways in which they can be used and also the effectiveness of how we use them and what paybacks we receive. The WHO Healthy Cities Project is, I think, a particularly vivid example of how the printed word, coupled with creative design and presentation, can be used most effectively (and cost effectively) to speed organizational networking. They have used a wide variety of such media. They have published a range of newsletters, some emanating from the hub of the network in WHO and some from different parts of the network, and the design of these has always been lively and well written, such that they invite people to scan them. Almost always there is mention of individual people in articles together with details of how to contact them. This mechanism, of course, provides widespread recognition of people's work, but also enables contacts to be made. Healthy Cities has also published a series of reports of a more technical nature that summarize the performance of individual Healthy Cities and make this information available to others. Their review of learning after the first two years had high-quality pictures, well-ordered and structured text and many interesting examples. Experience suggests that such printed media benefit from being professionally written, produced and edited in collaboration with insiders in order that their content is both appealing and continually reflecting the current issues travelling around the network. This requires people with energy and enthusiasm who can take on this journalistic role, working alongside media professionals.

Another simple media technology that is still little utilized in the context of organizations is the cassette audio tape. My consulting colleagues and I, who are located in different parts of England, have had good experiences using cassette tapes at times to communicate with each other. We have used these after attending a conference or a client visit to record our thoughts and feelings and thus be able to transmit to the others in the group a common message that they can listen to and reflect on in their own time. We thus avoid using expensive and precious meeting time for updating purposes.

In developing the KWS 2000 Pathfinder example, I was greatly helped in assembling material by Bram Breure in The Netherlands. He recorded his thoughts and impressions of the project on tape which provided a very good, practical basis for me to then write the story.

There must be many other creative ways to use this simple, cheap and very convenient technology in the context of organizational networking that remain yet to be pioneered. I look forward to hearing about examples of such uses.

Another technology that is becoming very widely used in organizations is video and videotape. With the advent of simple camcorders, video should take off further as a wonderfully informal means of building connections, relaying information and developing relationships within a network. Its immediacy and friendliness will, I believe, lead to an increasing number of creative uses being found for it in the years to come.

Branding and identity

'The media', as most of us now understand the phrase, have traditionally been used by public relations and corporate communications specialists to help create corporate identities. The issue of identity is no less important for the New

Organization, indeed its importance is bound to increase. I think, however, that it may be interpreted in some different ways.

Once again, the WHO Healthy Cities Project provides an example of a creative approach to the development of identity. Figure 5.1 showed a number of the logos of the 35 official Healthy Cities Projects. By taking a core idea (the number 2000, a silhouette and a particular typeface) and providing scope for each city to develop and interpret that idea to represent its own situation, the Healthy Cities Project has provided a potent visual image that both stresses a sense of collective purpose and identity while at the same time enabling individual autonomy and a sense of identity in particular elements within it.

This principle of simultaneous collectivity and autonomy will be an important one within the New Organization. No longer will we have the slavish implementation of the corporate logo that has been dictated from the centre; we will find ways of creating collective as well as local identity.

Once managers begin to see these soft technologies as an integrated range of tools for creating a foundation or infrastructure of personal interconnections that aids the organization's ability to feel small as it grows big, then they may start to take these tools more seriously, to invest in them more intelligently and with a greater clarity of purpose. They may also begin to weigh up more objectively their payback in relation to each other and to investment in hard communications technologies.

References

1 Kickbusch, Ilona (1989) 'Healthy Cities: a working project and a growing movement', Health Promotion 4, 2, pp 77–82.
2 Kickbusch, Ilona (1989) ibid.
3 Tsouros, Agis (Ed.) (1991) 'World Health Organization Healthy Cities Project: a project becomes a movement', WHO Regional Office for Europe, Copenhagen, Denmark.
4 Tsouros, Agis (Ed.) (1992) 'Twenty Steps for Developing a Healthy Cities Project', WHO Regional Office for Europe, Copenhagen, Denmark.
5 Barham, Kevin (1991) 'Networking—the corporate way round international discord', Multinational Business, No. 4, pp 1–11.
6 Grossman, Wendy (1991) 'Out of the Big Blue', Personal Computer World, VNU Business Publications, November, pp 162–166.
7 Copyright © 1988 of the Regents of the University of California. Reprinted by kind permission of the Regents. Christopher Bartlett and Sumantra Ghoshal (1988) 'Organizing for Worldwide Effectiveness: the Transnational Solution', California Management Review, 31, 1, Fall, pp 54–74.
8 Dumaine, Brian (1991) 'The Bureaucracy Busters', Fortune, June 17, pp 36–50.
9 Alpert, Mark (1991) 'Office Buildings for the 1990s', Fortune, November 18, pp 75–80.
10 Alpert, Mark (1991) ibid.

Ocean yachting

Imagine a fleet of sailing ships setting off on an expedition or race around the world. While these ships are in passage, they will meet many forces in their environment, some of which they have been able to prepare for and develop skills for dealing with, and others for which they will be quite unprepared. They will not be able to sail a straight course to their objective and, indeed, at times when the environment is particularly hazardous, they will change their objectives and head for a different port. Sometimes they will sail in convoy, but at other times they will take different routes, each using its skill to try to find the best way to reach port.

If these ships had been those of Columbus, then the uncertainties that they faced, the dangers with which they would have to deal and the capabilities they had for dealing with them would have been quite different from those of the modern ocean-going yachts. In the Whitbread Round the World Race, each of the yachts is a high-tech marvel—a highly developed technological and human machine, able to deal with some of the most extreme conditions imaginable. In addition, they have some stunning means of communication, not only with each other, but with land bases through the use of satellite communication technologies. Furthermore, if one can see these ships in the mind as a 'crowd of projects', each one traversing the oceans in a constant state of flux and adaptation to its environment, but at the same time held together with others by the invisible web of satellite communications and by a common purpose, perhaps one has a picture of the New Organization.

6
Project working—how to implement widespread teamworking

PATHFINDER
KWS 2000

A network of environmental projects

Pollution, like networking, knows no boundaries. For a country like The Netherlands, which lies at a major geographical crossroads, pollution is generated internally and both exported and imported via river systems, the sea and air currents. Since the early 1980s, The Netherlands has been a leader in the implementation of far-sighted environmental policies. However, in the late 1980s, in a fundamental review of their policies, they determined to take a much more pro-active and integrated approach to environmental problems, both within the country itself and in influencing these matters at a European and international level.

In analysing the multiple causes of pollution, and their limited success in curbing the problem in the early 1980s, they quickly realized that it was no good tackling just one source or diminishing one effect without simultaneously tackling other sources and other effects. All were interrelated. Without a total view and an integrated programme, the solution to one part of the problem frequently resulted in merely passing the problem further up or down the eco-chain.[1]

The problem facing the Government (as indeed all governments when it comes to environmental problems) is, however, a massive one. How do you make the large numbers of people and vested interests who both contribute to environmental problems and can play a role in solving them, act in concert towards environmental goals and, in the end, change their current practices and behaviour? Equally, how do you motivate people today to tackle problems the benefits of which may only be seen in 25 or more years' time?

The approach being taken in The Netherlands is comprehensive. It involves, first, the participation and contribution of many different government depart-

102

ments and agencies, at national and local levels. It also involves key target economic groupings, such as agriculture, traffic and transport, the building trade, consumers and different industrial sectors. The overarching mechanism chosen to implement the policy on such a broad front is the environmental programme—a giant network of environmental programmes and projects.

Its aim is to have the country's environmental problems under control within 20 years. Within the overall programme, there are many subsidiary programmes and, within those, there are projects and subsequent projects within projects. In some ways this hierarchy of projects is very ordered, very disciplined and clearly organized, but in others it builds in a large number of links between different subprojects simply as a result of the highly interrelated nature of environmental problems.

KWS 2000 is one such subproject. It focuses on problems of air pollution and, specifically, those problems caused by the waste and diffusion of organic solvents into the atmosphere from industry and consumer sources. (Those emissions from agriculture and traffic are dealt with in other programmes). KWS 2000 typifies some of the project and networking structures and processes that have now been reproduced many hundreds of times in the first stages of implementing The Netherlands' environmental policy.

Consensus building

It has been a fundamental belief of the environmental policy throughout that it is only when there is active involvement and participation of large numbers of those with vested interests that significant progress can be made in the long term. KWS 2000 has used an explicit process of extensive consensus building among these different parties. This process emphasizes open discussion, avoiding defensive attitudes, joint work on problem solving and finding common goals. Considerable effort has gone into negotiations aimed at gaining commitment to the ways in which the policy is to be implemented. There is no doubt that it has to be implemented eventually because of the range of legislative goals, financial incentives and other sanctions put in place to support it. The main issue, though, is to ensure widespread, consistent and, as far as possible, rapid implementation.

Structuring the network

The KWS 2000 programme is project managed out of the Air Department of the Ministry of the Environment. The programme has four key partners (note the use of the word partner, which is important symbolically). The first partner is the national government, which has an important vested interest and, indeed, responsibility to ensure achievement of environmental goals. The second group of partners is the 12 provincial authorities in The Netherlands. Third partners are industry as a whole. At this stage of implementation, the industry group is further split into specific industry sectors according to the sector organizations and companies collaborating on the project. Finally, the fourth group of partners is the local municipalities within The Netherlands.

These four partners are represented on the two major coordinating mechanisms. The first group, known as the Steering Group, is very much responsible for the overall policy of KWS 2000. Its role is strategic. It decides the general direction of implementation and meets twice a year. The second level, the Project Group or project management team, is responsible for the monitoring of progress across the range of activities. It meets 5–7 times a year. Supporting these three levels is a permanent Project Bureau, resourced by the Ministry of the Environment and responsible for the day-to-day coordination of activities at all levels. Part of the role of the Project Bureau is to be aware of the range of resources and expertise that they can draw on within The Netherlands and beyond both for their specific field and other projects. They have, therefore, their internal project network to facilitate as well as their wider external network. In particular, they have made links with government bodies and industrial organizations in other countries in order to learn from them and to influence their activities and policies in the light of The Netherlands' experience. To this end, they organized the first International Congress on solvent emissions in Maastricht and sent five KWS 'missions' to Sweden, Norway, Denmark, Germany and Switzerland to explain the aims and methods of KWS 2000. They also, in turn, of course, draw on the networks of those people participating in the working groups and taskforces with the enormous multiplier effect that this brings. Their crucial role is to provide the environment in which these people will feel motivated to provide their time and energy.

Subprojects

Flowing from the formal project goals and implementation plans developed by the Steering and Project groups, KWS 2000 further splits down into 15 subprojects, called Taskforces. Each of these works at an operational level and is responsible for implementation in a particular sector. These Taskforces draw on volunteers from companies, from provincial and national government and from other sources of technical or research support contributing their expertise as required.

A second major type of subproject resulting from the implementation plans is generated in the provinces. Each province agrees a range of specific objectives aimed at focusing and speeding up implementation in its particular geographical area. It also agrees a system for monitoring progress against overall goals and against the implementation plan itself. Once again, these provincial projects, while more heavily staffed by the provincial authorities, will also draw on a wide range of expertise, depending on the nature of the problems addressed by each project. Provinces also bring an added dimension because it is they who provide companies in their areas a licence to operate. They are, therefore, in a position to negotiate positively with companies about their environmental programmes.

Network communications

To some people, KWS 2000 may look like just another hierarchical, bureaucratic type of organization. Closer inspection shows, however, that most of its activity and progress depends on relationships with no direct line of authority. It relies for the most part on mobilizing voluntary effort. It cannot rely on formal authority, nor does it exercise any control over most of its resources. It does have the power of negative sanction in the form of legislation, but chooses not to use this as the main instrument for achieving its goals. Indeed, KWS 2000 was started with the explicit aim of avoiding legislation where possible simply because the process of drafting and enacting legislation is so slow that visible results would certainly not come before the year 2000. The national government, however, can still use the big stick of the law in the last resort where a particular sector, for example, is unwilling to implement the policy.

Given the enormous complexity and diversity of parties involved in the project, and that, at least in its present form, it has a finite timescale in which to achieve its particular goals (the year 2000, the process having been initiated in 1986), it is not surprising that most of the communication comes in the low-tech, soft category. There are clearly some impediments to investing in the high-tech in this kind of situation, unless, as with France's Minitel, there is a standardized national electronic network that anyone can access easily. The role of the Project Bureau, which in some ways acts as the spider in the middle of the web, catching and pulling necessary resources, appears to be critical. It provides the strong reminder of purpose and mission enshrined in the national policy, while also providing a framework for action in the form of a project implementation plan that binds the activities of many different people together.

In the project startup phase, when the joint development of the implementation plans with the four main partners was particularly crucial, the Project Bureau sponsored a number of workshops that were important in the building up of commitment to the final implementation routes chosen. These workshops used the consensus building method, with external consultants acting as facilitators. They created a critical mass of people from the different partners who had contributed to the final plan and who subsequently acted as ambassadors as the plan unfolded.

In the implementation stages, the major communication need has been to disseminate ideas, solutions, lessons learned and problems experienced around the total multiproject network as rapidly as possible. To enable this, the Project Bureau (acting as one hub) has been the sponsor of a number of workshops, theme days, annual reports and reports of demonstration projects that have been made widely available. The other major communications hubs have tended to be industry sector bodies who disseminated solutions found to work in one company so that these could be applied in other companies. Industry working groups have also been prolific in producing factsheets, running industry seminars and courses and publishing the findings of working groups in relevant industry journals. While many of the activities are sector specific, where solutions or problems are common to two or more sectors, the Project Bureau creates both formal and *ad hoc* mechanisms for such knowledge to be exchanged. There has also been an attempt to create an electronic bulletin board system for exchanging emerging know-how, but this has not yet really taken off. Industry sector bodies have also been instrumental in obtaining and sharing know-how from their counterparts in other European countries in order to ensure widespread awareness and application of current best practice.

Left out and behind

The major difficulty experienced by KWS 2000 to date is the problem of really engaging the 650 municipalities. While the provincial authorities can deal with some of the larger companies in each sector, as do the relevant sector organizations, it is through the municipalities that the smaller, local industries can be accessed by local licensing arrangements. While there seems to be a culture that has been developed between government, the provinces and industry based on a highly pro-active, influencing role, this approach is not shared by the municipalities.

This seems partly to be because of the very limited resources they were able to commit to the startup and implementation stages of the project, but also due to a culture clash between the pro-active nature of the project as a whole (and, in particular, towards licensing companies) and the more bureaucratic views encountered in the municipalities. They want to be able to apply a standardized procedure to every company rather than to get into an active influencing and debating role with each of them about how they should be implementing KWS 2000.

Steps have now been taken to help the municipalities catch up with information, but the attitudinal problem persists. The question that this raises, therefore, is whether KWS 2000 may run out of steam or need added boosts of energy if it is to achieve its objectives on a wide scale in the time envisaged.

Conclusion

KWS 2000 is a good example of a programme approach, containing within it multiple-focused projects as well as a certain degree of fluidity and flexibility as new problems and initiatives constantly come up. Its combination of hard project definitions and monitoring approaches gives it a rigour that is counterbalanced by its recognition that it can only implement these projects using softer approaches that are designed to engage the motivation, interest and involvement of many people. They offer their services to the whole in exchange for obtaining benefit for themselves and their companies.

At the same time, by casting its net extremely widely beyond its hub in the Air Ministry in order to find its resources, it creates and mobilizes a breathtakingly large series of overlapping networks that are held together by a clear, common purpose, soft technology and the veiled threat of legislative sanctions.

> We had the technical capability to progress almost any human resource problem—either ourselves or via formal and informal networks. What we lacked was the project capability which would enable us to define a problem in a way the business understood it and to gain commitment to the aims whilst effectively managing the political, social and cultural variables of implementing the changes.
>
> Bill Thurston, Personnel Director, Home Services Division,
> Prudential Corporation

1   Team working by means of projects

On one characteristic of the New Organization just about all the management theorists agree: the central role of multidisciplinary teams and projects as a way of getting things done. Tom Peters,[2] Peter Drucker,[3] The MIT study of management in the 1990s[4] and many others all point to the role that such groupings will have.

The resulting organization can be conceived of as a constantly changing kaleidoscope of teams, forming, delivering work and dissolving as required. Hans Mikkelsen, a Danish consultant, calls this the 'crowd of projects'. I like the feeling of bustle in his image.

The essence of these teams is that they are multifunctional, multidisciplinary and frequently multilocational and multicountry. When you look at the traditional type of organization chart you probably cannot 'see' them. They are composed of individuals who may be positioned anywhere either within or even outside the organization. They are, in this sense, invisible teams. We might imagine them as being marked on any organizational chart in ultraviolet pen that, when shone under ultraviolet light reveals them to be in some way interconnected to perform a particular task. Quinn Mills, Professor of Business Administration at the Harvard Business School, has called them 'clusters'.[5] It is a good word as it suggests assembling different groupings or constellations of people from different places for different purposes. The word, I gather, originated in IBM.

The tasks that these clusters or teams take on are increasingly described and defined as projects. Using project thinking ensures that the teams' tasks are clear and focused and that timescales, resources and constraints are clearly understood by all, thus introducing clear accountability and a results orientation.

The key criterion for assembling these teams using people in multiple networks becomes that of relevant expertise, experience and potential contribution and not role, status or representation. This is a fundamental concept of great importance. You pull people together because of what they can *contribute* and not because of *who* they are. They exercise quality control primarily by means of interaction and critique from their peers who are in the best place to judge their work and not so much from their superiors. They set many of their own goals within the overall strategy and mission of the organization. They are given autonomy, but they also accept accountability and responsibility.

Such team working, allied to the project way of thinking, are the New Organization's primary mechanisms for ensuring high performance. High performance stems from bringing together the right mix of brain power, focusing that brain power on complicated problems and the collective commitment to results that flow from effective teamwork and project management. Many organizations use teams and projects but few know how to get real performance out of them. The vast majority underperform.

The key applications

Clearly however not *every* task requires great groups of people coordinated in a complicated way to achieve it. We should not fall into the trap of believing that *everything* in the New Organization has to be done using the teamworking route. Many are still achieved by means of a more traditional line function.

How, though, do you decide when it is particularly appropriate? It works particularly well in two major areas. The first is in relation to operational business processes, such as the integration of a coordinated customer service across different functions or the process of delivering consistent quality to customers. In short, any operational element that is part of the business process which satisfies customers by its very nature involves the input of many different functions. Teamworking is critical at such times. There is currently a lot of work taking place in this area under the general title of business process re-engineering, which is redesigning such operational processes to bring together the role of IT and teamworking.

At the other end of the spectrum, there are some important processes to do with the strategy and development of the business and the organization, that is, those processes which in some way shape its future. Once again, these are, by their nature, highly complicated and require the building of a critical mass of people who can commit round an emerging consensus. Increasingly, such New Organizations are using multiple team-based project approaches in the development and implementation of their strategies. One such company is Neste OY, the major oil company in Finland, which has used large numbers of taskforces and project teams among its senior managers and operating units as a mechanism for refocusing its business after the major political changes in eastern bloc countries and the deregulation of its home market. Boards and senior teams who try to cling on to the notion that strategy is their job, and theirs alone, are doomed.

New product development is another area that benefits particularly from the teamworking approach. Unless most companies radically improve their ability to bring more new products to the market more rapidly, they will lose out. Lyons Tetley, a UK-based food and beverage group selling throughout the world, has seen the benefits of using project teams as a mechanism for bringing new products onto the market rapidly. What they have also realized, wisely, is that their organization had to work in a different way in order to make this happen. That requires the right structures and processes, not just product ideas or technologies.

The changing role of the personnel function is another area that is asking for a teamworking approach. As the personnel role moves from being a reactive protector of the current rules and regulations towards being a more dynamic force in the management of change within the organization, not only do the different specialisms within personnel need to integrate their efforts more closely, but they have to work much more in tandem with their clients and partners within the business.

Finally, there is an area where the approach is appropriate, but is very underutilized. That is the preparation and implementation of acquisitions and mergers. Much of the appallingly high failure rate in this area is due to the inability of management to create processes that integrate different cultures and systems rapidly enough in order to realize desirable synergies. Most players in the acquisition game pay scant attention to integration processes, seduced by the thrill of the chase and the acquisition, but bored by the much more painstaking task of crafting a successful new organization out of previously separate ones. Cross-company integration projects implemented rapidly in the early days are an important mechanism that make this merging process produce pay-offs more rapidly.

Using the project approach

While I am advocating throughout this book that organizations invest in helping people to build up their social networks both inside and outside the organization, putting in place infrastructures to help this, and while I believe strongly that the tissue of organizational networking is the roots of the New Organization, it is not there as an end in itself. It is there as a powerful response mechanism to enable resources to be focused rapidly, efficiently and effectively on to objectives, goals and tasks. This is most usually and easily done in connection with a task of some kind. Tasks are the basis for cooperation and interaction between people. Many tasks can be carried out by just two people in this manner.

However, more complicated tasks require a greater input of know-how and representation and they may take a long time to carry out. It is in these larger tasks that the marriage between a teamworking mentality and project thinking comes into its own. The project approach originated in industries such as construction where complicated tasks could be planned in great detail, often with the help of specialized project-planning software and built using experience of the past as a guide to the estimation of time and resources required. For many of the major tasks that the New Organization has to carry out, this particular mechanistic approach to project management is not appropriate, but an adaptation of some of the core ideas behind project management applied to this new situation is very pertinent.

Simple precepts of the project approach are that it identifies clear goals and the scope of the work, identifies the resources that are to be committed to the achievement of those goals, monitors progress against agreed milestones and timescales and reviews progress regularly as a mechanism for adaptation to changing circumstances. In two previous books written with colleagues, *Superteams*[6] and *Project Leadership*[7] there is more detail on how such project thinking can be adapted to the requirements of the New Organization. An example of how the project approach may be applied is given in Box 6.1.

Box 6.1   The Prudential Corporation—Project Octopus

Home Services, the major business division of the Prudential Corporation, one of the giants of the UK insurance industry, faced with an increasingly competitive market-place, went about a massive restructuring and refocusing of its business.

An important element of this was the reorientation of the skills and attitudes of a massive sales force that had been operating in much the same way for a long time and needed to become much more professional in its selling techniques.

This change process, itself designed as a project with a cross-disciplinary team, together with other projects that were involved with the overall change process, made significant new demands on the roles of the 120-strong personnel function. While, in the words of one of the personnel specialists, 'personnel's role historically was to police an environment that sought stability', personnel's role now was to be one of the major drivers and partners in the implementation of change in the business.

In operational terms, this required not only teamworking between personnel and a variety of functions within different parts of the business, but also a much greater interdependence among previously separate personnel specialisms. Where projects had been carried out, some had not always been successful. The Personnel Director's analysis was that they suffered from:

- inadequacies of scope and, in particular, a tendency to set briefs too narrowly in personnel terms rather than organizational and business terms
- insufficient attention given to recognizing different priorities and gaining the commitment of multiple stakeholders.

His answer was a development and change programme, codenamed Project Octopus, which pulled together a number of development strands over a period of two years.

Two key roles in personnel were seen as being instrumental in creating both a project culture and wideranging project capability. Members of the senior team needed to develop the new attitudes and skills of being 'project sponsors' rather than line managers. Work was done with them to introduce them to this role and coach them in its application. In parallel, groups of actual and potential project leaders were identified. They embarked on a series of modular development programmes in which they learnt about various aspects of project working, applied those to their projects and then reviewed their successes and failures collectively and individually, with consultants acting as mentors. The first group of project leaders also developed a booklet designed as a set of working principles, a common language and an introduction to project working that could be widely disseminated and used, even by those people not coming on the initial programmes.

Spin-offs from these programmes highlighted key blockages in managing the portfolio of projects. The division as a whole was trying to undertake too much and was not prioritizing its objectives sufficiently. A new project team analysed the situation and, in conjunction with the senior team, put new management processes in place. These included formalization of some simple project disciplines such as defining their scope, project review meetings, work breakdowns and internal marketing plans that sponsors would require of project leaders.

2   Practical project problems

However many writers, theorists and managers advocate teamworking, I find that few even question the likely effectiveness and success of teamworking approaches. It seems to be regarded as a self-evident truth that by bringing people together, effective teams and projects will ensue. The mythology of the highly successful and powerful multidisciplinary team is fostered by some extraordinary success stories.[8] Each company has its conspicuous success stories, but does not talk about its failures. There is a romance about the success stories, for there is no doubt that when a multidisciplinary team works, it is capable of going quite beyond the limits of the possible. However, in reality, the picture of success is considerably more patchy. There are real problems that need paying attention to if the benefits of team and project working are to be fully realized.

Conflicting expectations

Project teams are located in an organizational context in which they are meeting the expectations of multiple, not single, stakeholders and clients, many of whose requirements are at odds with each other. In order to get their work done, the team has to be perceived as consisting not only of the core or visible team members but of a whole range of 'invisible' team members who, in some way, can and must contribute to the successful accomplishment of the task.

This wider sense of what Damien Synnott[9] of OTR, a London and Brussels-based IT research organization, calls 'the extended team' comes from taking into account all of those who have expertise that may be relevant, expectations of the outcomes of the project or the ability to impede its progress. Add to this potent cocktail of complexity the fact that these teams now consist of individualists—call them prima donnas if you will—with strong egos, strong opinions and a desire for autonomy as well as a desire to contribute to a team.

Worlds apart

A further reality is that, working on a global scale, these teams may seldom actually come together to produce our traditional view of the team working in a room together round a table. They are teams apart.[10] This clearly makes getting together more difficult and means that communication has to rely on the various hard and soft technologies. As one project manager described it to me, 'I find that unless I can pull all these people together at least once every three months we get drift, however carefully we have spelled out everybody's roles, responsibilities and deadlines in between times'. There is a continual danger that out of sight becomes out of mind. Key members *literally* forget that they are members of a team. They forget the existence of the other people who are dependent on them and on whom they depend.

It is also a sad but true fact that simply putting a multidisciplinary group of individuals together and giving them a task does not create a team. Different disciplines and expertise literally use different languages to understand the world. Even within the *same* discipline, specialists often cannot understand each other. It is not surprising, then, that multidisciplinary teams start off with communication problems that inhibit their ability to quickly gel into a high-performance unit. Cultural differences also increasingly play a part in causing difficulties. These may be cultures derived from nationality where quite different world views have to be understood, tolerated and worked with. The cultures may be derived from organizations, coming together in joint ventures and strategic alliances or organizations such as suppliers and their customers linking themselves together for joint projects. Here, again, very different organizational cultures can have difficulty understanding each other. ABB, as we have seen, is highly aware of the work and skills that are needed to create organizations capable of handling these issues fluently.

Ineffectual meetings

Even when teams can come together, it is commonly felt that meetings are too long, unrewarding and unproductive. It is incredible that, even in sophisticated international organizations, the basic skills of running effective meetings are still not practiced in a widespread manner. This is not only a vast waste of time and money, it is also sad because, for many team members, this is how they remember the team. Yet many managers will not vote funds for meetings training—they still, amazingly, see it as a cost rather than investment. Team-working is more difficult than individual working and it has to bring rewards to individuals if they are to continue to make the necessary investment in the team.

Looking outwards

One of the other dangers that besets many such teams is that of becoming excessively inward-looking. They easily forget that they are highly dependent on and interdependent with the rest of the organization, beyond which their 'customers' reside and their performance will be judged. It also from here that many of their resources and support will have to come. The New Organization will accentuate this issue.

Teams that do not continually look outwards as well as inwards fail to understand the shifting nature of the organization's politics and the dynamics and sensitivities of different people and groups to what they are doing. Their environments too will always be fast-changing and uncertain, where the goalposts may be moving and the political quicksands of the organization shift in real time. However brilliantly they organize themselves and plan or their technical solutions to the problems posed, if they fail to carry at least a critical mass of people in the organization and the wider external stakeholders along with them, then they fail.

They also have to manage many other factors that at first sight are beyond their control. For example, the organization (in practice this usually means senior management or project sponsors) is frequently not prepared to take enough time to work with the project team so that it becomes absolutely clear about why it wants the project. Unless the project team is very persistent in extracting this clarity, it frequently sets itself up to fail right from the outset. It can also fall victim to management's inability to create effective processes for prioritization and resource allocation between different projects. Senior management can also unwittingly derail project teams by appointing the wrong person to the project leadership role. I and others have found that one of the most common causes of failure is where the person is put into the project leader role by virtue of their technical ability without any thought being given to the managerial and organizational complexity of this role and the skills and competences required. Likewise, senior management in their sponsor role can cause the failure of projects when they lose their nerve when the going gets tough. This is just when the project needs their added leadership, advocacy and support.

The other tough problem is for team members in this new kind of environment. It is a relative luxury for an individual to be assigned full time to a project team. Most people are members of several project groups or clusters. In addition, they may have line, operational or process responsibilities of a routine nature. The pressures and stresses of conflicting objectives and priorities on people are very real and frequently ignored in these situations.

So, the pressures and problems are real, but not insoluble. Clarifying senior management's role and preparing people with new skills will produce the desired benefits.

3   Successful project working

Managing the projects portfolio

An organization consisting of a fluid and constantly changing mix of large and small projects involving different groupings of people at different times presents senior management with new challenges in capacity planning, prioritization and monitoring.

The project slate

Without the strong planning and control processes of the bureaucratic organization, how do you work out how many people you need and ensure that the people that you have are not overloaded?

In the New Organization much of this has to come from the people themselves taking responsibility for estimating and bidding for resources and also managing their own time. However, there are some things that senior management should do on their part to create the context within which this can easily happen.

One of the basic tools is what is known in some organizations as the 'project slate'. This is a visible manifestation of the portfolio of projects that are in progress at any one time. It is clearly a part of senior management's role to be managing this portfolio. It does this by ensuring that projects link to strategy, allocating shifting priorities and resources between projects, ensuring projects are reviewed or sometimes closed down and ensure that simple project disciplines are observed. It must also ensure that the whole organization learns from successes and mistakes in individual projects. It is crucial, however, that these do not become heavily bureaucratic processes. It is here that the new technologies can be particularly helpful in achieving this, as the story in Box 6.2 illustrates.

Box 6.2   Keeping your eye on multiple projects

> So here you are in the year 2000, and you've got a constantly changing, adaptive organization. How will you keep track of all this chaos? At Cypress Semiconductor, CEO TJ Rodgers has a computer system that allows him to stay abreast of every employee and team in his fast-moving, decentralized, constantly changing organization. Each employee maintains a list of 10 to 15 goals . . . Noted next to each goal is when it was agreed upon, when it's due to be finished and whether it's finished yet or not.
>
> This way it doesn't take layers of expensive bureaucracy to check who's doing what, whether someone has got a light enough workload to be put on a new team and who's having trouble. Rodgers says he can review the goals of all 1500 employees in about four hours, which he does each week. He looks only for those falling behind, and then calls not to scold but to ask if there's anything he can do to help them get the job done. On the surface the system may seem bureaucratic but it takes only about a half hour a week for employees to review and update their lists.
>
> Brian Dumaine, *Fortune*[11]

Senior management's role is not to do the work, but to act as a lighthouse, continuously guiding the project towards its organizational goals, helping it to avoid organizational rocks and ensuring that it has the necessary support and resources to be successful.

New rules of assembly

As a manager of organizational networking, you must keep an eye open for the underlying rules of assembly. In the traditional organization, how people are invited to join a team, a taskforce or a working group is usually fairly obvious. It is based heavily on role and position, as well as on principles of representation. The key criterion for assembling teams from multiple networks becomes, instead, that of relevant expertise and experience. This is a fundamental concept of great importance. You pull people together because of what they can contribute and not because of their status.

It is very easy for the old rules of assembly to carry over imperceptibly into the new situation: the same faces turn up at the same meetings and appear in many different groupings. It must be said, too, that the same can happen in the more advanced and sophisticated networked organizations. It often happens that those who are the most visible, the most energetic, the most enthusiastic and the most successful get asked to contribute disproportionately in many different areas. This is not only dangerous in the long term for them, but it is dangerous for the organization as a whole for one of the New Organization's principles is that it is continually providing opportunities for a *range* of talent to display itself. It is continually looking for fresh thinking by bringing people with different skills and so on to bear on projects. Therefore, whatever the stage of development of your organization, pay attention to whether there are some invisible unwritten rules that limit the membership of key groupings to a small élite club of people. Be aware, however, that even if you believe this opening up to be beneficial, others will also be resistant to it. Extending membership makes life less comfortable.

There are several ways in which this can be done. How many organizations, for example, are yet comfortable with including their clients and their suppliers on their in-company training courses? How many use their external consultants and subcontractors to sit on internal project groupings as permanent members for the duration of a project? How many of them put young and inexperienced people into important task groups to accelerate their development and widen their understanding and appreciation of how the organization works and how to get things done within it? Frequently, of course, it is these most unlikely sources that are able to ask the dumb question or suggest the radical solution, often imported from a totally different field.

Training and development

Developing all-round project capability is a complicated process that evolves over a considerable period of time. The aim is to have people who can slot in very quickly to multidisciplinary project teams and have the necessary know-how and a common project language to start working effectively. It is also character-ized by a range of supporting systems and management processes that are required to support the project way of working.

Four targets for project training

There are four main roles that, ideally, need to be involved in the training and development processes. First is the important role of project sponsor—the person who is senior management's advocate and supporter of the project as well as the person who represents the organization's requirements of that project.

The second critical grouping is of those people who are (or who are likely to become) project leaders. As already mentioned, these people, particularly if they have technical backgrounds, are frequently ill-prepared for such roles. Figure 6.1 serves as a framework for developing the skills of people who have to undertake the complicated role of managing projects within the challenging conditions of fluid, flexible organizations.

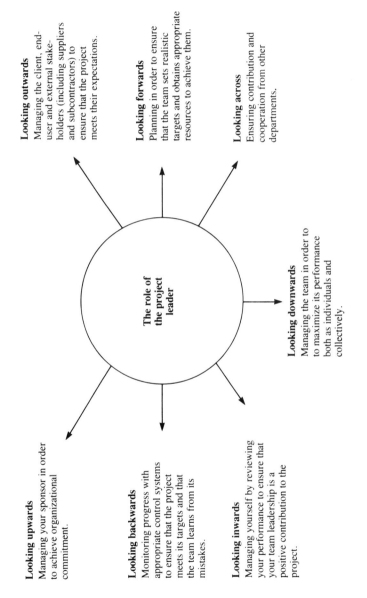

Looking outwards
Managing the client, end-user and external stake-holders (including suppliers and subcontractors) to ensure that the project meets their expectations.

Looking forwards
Planning in order to ensure that the team sets realistic targets and obtains appropriate resources to achieve them.

Looking across
Ensuring contribution and cooperation from other departments.

The role of the project leader

Looking downwards
Managing the team in order to to maximize its performance both as individuals and collectively.

Looking upwards
Managing your sponsor in order to achieve organizational commitment.

Looking backwards
Monitoring progress with appropriate control systems to ensure that the project meets its targets and that the team learns from its mistakes.

Looking inwards
Managing yourself by reviewing your performance to ensure that your team leadership is a positive contribution to the project.

Figure 6.1 The project leader's direction finder (from *Project Leadership* by Wendy Briner, Mike Geddes and Colin Hastings, Gower, 1990).

The third grouping is the clients and the users of projects. Depending on the nature of the organization, these may be within the business or externally in other organizations. One thing, however, is clear—clients and users are key team members. Their input and contribution in terms of ideas and helping to keep things on track become extremely important. They need to understand the way the project team is working. They need to understand how they can contribute to its success, which is in their best interests and, therefore, they need to be included in training and development activities.

The fourth grouping that frequently gets involved is the key service providers within the organization. It is these people who provide contributions, not necessarily as part of the core project team, but contributions that, nevertheless, are vitally important at different stages. They are part of the team by virtue of being only occasionally involved, but, because they are not there all the time this means that they can occasionally slip up. Likewise, they must be participants in training courses and workshops, not only to develop their skills, but so that they can be effectively networked into the organization.

Mentoring

Sponsors should keep a weather eye on key individuals who may become overloaded. As mentioned earlier, effective people tend to have too many demands made of them. It should not be underestimated how difficult it is, particularly for younger people, to manage the stress that comes from competing demands of roles that they may have in different project groupings. Coaching and mentoring, both by project leaders and sponsors, is a good way to help them work through ways in which to resolve these issues, for within the New Organization it is they themselves who will actually have to take responsibility for this.

Cross-cultural issues

Issues of cross-cultural working are now being tackled increasingly by means of cross-cultural workshops and cultural awareness training. We are now beginning to have a much better understanding of the ways in which different countries' cultures are different and have an impact in the work-place.[13] For me this is not a *problem*, but, instead, one of the most exciting aspects of the world of the twenty-first century that will impact many of us. Businesses and other working organizations that span different cultures and can foster cooperative working towards common tasks and goals, have an enormous role to play in creating a new world order.

Many of our Pathfinders, such as the WHO Healthy Cities Project, Digital and ABB seem very clear about the importance of valuing such diversity and building into the organization's culture not only an acceptance of differences, but the positive ability to turn them to good effect. Projects are one of the vehicles organizations will use to bring this about.

In the first instance, cross-cultural project working may only affect relatively small groups of people, but, as our Pathfinders' experience demonstrates, there can be no doubt that this will accelerate rapidly over the years to come, even if much of that project working happens between teams that seldom, if ever, actually meet face to face.

Through these development processes and systems each organization will evolve its own way of managing projects successfully. There can be no set formulae that can be applied uncritically to every situation. Each organization will use different language and will find different factors that are particularly important in creating high-performance project teams.

References

1 'Environmental Policy in The Netherlands', Ministerie van Volkshuisvesting, The Hague, The Netherlands.
2 Peters, Tom and Robert Waterman (1982) *In Search of Excellence*, Harper & Row, New York.
3 Copyright © (1988) of the President and Fellows of Harvard College; all rights reserved. Reprinted by permission of *Harvard Business Review*. Peter Drucker (1988) 'The Coming of the New Organization', *Harvard Business Review*; January–February, pp 45–53.
4 Ernst and Young (1989), 'The Landmark MIT Study: management in the 1990s', Ernst and Young Consultants, New York, USA.
5 Copyright © (1988) of the President and Fellows of Harvard College; all rights reserved. Reprinted by permission of *Harvard Business Review*. Lynda Applegate, James Cash and D Quinn Mills (1988) 'Information Technology and Tomorrow's Manager', *Harvard Business Review*, November–December, pp 128–136.
6 Hastings, Colin, Peter Bixby and Rani Chaudhry-Lawton (1986) *Superteams*, Fontana, London.
7 Briner, Wendy, Michael Geddes and Colin Hastings (1990) *Project Leadership*, Gower, England.
8 The following books tell good stories about high performing teams: Tracy Kidder (1981) *The Soul of a New Machine*, Little, Brown & Co., Boston; Norman Mailer (1970) *Of a Fire on the Moon*, Little, Brown & Co., Boston; and John Sculley (1988) *Odyssey: Pepsi to Apple*, Collins, London.
9 Synnott, Damien (1990) 'Project Rescue in IT', OTR Client Forum, London.
10 Hastings, Colin *et al.* (1986) ibid.
11 Dumaine, Brian (1991) 'The Bureaucracy Busters', *Fortune*, June 19, pp 36–50.
12 Briner, Wendy *et. al.* (1990) ibid.
13 Hofstede, Geert (1991) *Cultures and Organizations*, McGraw-Hill, London.

**Pictures in
the mind**

Gardening

An appealingly different image has been adopted by Norsk Hydro, the Norwegian utilities company. They have likened their organization to a garden in which the people of the organization are the flowers. This is a very rich image that helps us to see the organization as fertile ground in which people grow, develop and collectively produce something of profound satisfaction for all those who come across it. It reminds me of a talk I had not very long ago with Alan Bryant, the head of gardens at Ashridge, the international business school north of London, who was the only person in the organization who had a very clear 25-year strategic plan for his part of the business!

There are very many other good sub elements to the image, too. What about cross-pollination within the organization, for example, fertilization of ideas, bearing fruit and so on. There is also the idea that you have to prepare the ground before plants will grow, but that fertilizer, water and sunshine are required for healthy growth. Gardens, too, can become overgrown and at times need organizing or pruning back.

7
Sharing know-how—how to maximize the return on your key asset

PATHFINDER
The BP HSE Technology Team

The aftermath of an acquisition is seldom the most fertile breeding ground for subsequent collaboration and networking. Indeed, it frequently creates their opposites: suspicion wariness, turf battles and competition for scarce resources. These are the very antitheses of the synergy that the protagonists of the acquisition usually put forward to justify it in the first place.

Like every other company before it, BP experienced some of these problems following its merger with Standard Oil in America. One of the issues of concern related to technology provision to BP's businesses. Hitherto, Standard Oil had worked closely with its Warrensville research centre and BP with its Sunbury research centre and with its Engineering Department. The Standard Oil research labs were based at Warrensville, a suburb of Cleveland, in Ohio. BP's main UK research labs were based in Sunbury on the south eastern outer rim of London. BP's engineering services, at that time, were also based in London. In addition, there were various small, technical groupings within the new corporate centre in the city of London. In recent years, BP's engineering services moved to Uxbridge, giving a wider geographical spread for technology provision.

The vision

For a number of years after the merger, difficulties in achieving commonality of purpose and view still existed. However, a number of factors within BP caused some key players within these units to start rethinking and initiate a search for ways to improve the situation.

On the one hand BP's wider culture change process, Project 1990, had begun to stress the important role of multidisciplinary and cross-location teams as a mechanism for getting things done. In addition, each of these units was operating in a much tougher environment. They have to pay their way by selling their services to their customers—the three major BP businesses. When asked, the businesses expressed disquiet about the apparent duplication and lack of coordination between the different sites. They were complaining that, at times, they received competing bids from different sites and that on projects they, the customer, frequently had to coordinate the activities of different elements being done for them by the different sites.

The Project 1990 process had also made very explicit BP's desire to be seen as a world leader in its approach to environmental and safety problems—both of them being crucial issues facing the oil industry and having fundamental impacts on the bottom line. Empowerment and networking were also encouraged and, as the management of the technology function began to change, the culture change ideas began to be translated into action.

Previously informal discussions had taken place between people in the different sites about the next stages in realizing this strategy. It gradually emerged that, in all of them, there was a growing desire for greater links between sites and dissatisfaction with the status quo.

These discussions began to focus on a broad vision of integrating the HSE resources in the three main locations into an international team able to coordinate its activities and resources in the service of the businesses. In order to try and move things forward, two managers (with the encouragement of relevant senior management) agreed to fund a workshop. This brought together 18 key people from the three main sites, together with representatives from other areas concerned, in order to explore this concept, to see whether commitment to it existed and what might be necessary to make it happen if, indeed, it was thought to be feasible.

Planning and learning together

The process of the workshop was, at times, challenging and exhilarating as the three groups came together face to face for the first time. They rapidly discovered how little they knew about each other. Stereotypes and misperceptions that had arisen about the role, expertise, goals and motives of each began to emerge.

Speaking some previously unspoken thoughts became the basis for more honest talking, the removal of previous distrust and the gradual building of productive relationships between the parties. The result of this process was that the different parties were able to see each other's strengths and weaknesses more objectively and build respect for and appreciation of the talents that each group might bring to the overall team. Also, thought was given as to how these talents might complement each other rather than necessarily compete with each other.

At times it looked as though the process might break down as the different groups experienced the very real difficulty of reaching a common view. My role as one of the consultants was to allow them to come to the brink of failure, but not to allow them to fail. Participants felt strongly that going so close to the edge together was a crucial element in finally bringing about agreement on the need for a common approach.

An important element of the workshop involved bringing in senior representatives from the major BP businesses so that they, too, could contribute their perceptions of the different parties within the embryonic international HSE technology team. They were briefed not to mince their words and did not.

They thought that the international team, once integrated, could offer a world-beating resource to meet their needs. Above all, however, the businesses endorsed and lent their support to the concept of an integrated team, with the result that they, the clients, could go 'one-stop shopping'. In other words, through one point of contact they could access the full resource base of all the sites and those people's activities coordinated by the HSE team itself in order to solve business problems and be confident that the best people would be found. Throughout the rest of the workshop the business representatives joined the other delegates and made substantial contributions to the refinement of the ideas as well as invaluable advice on how to sell them to the businesses more widely.

Outcomes

The consequence of the workshop was a much stronger level of commitment among the group of 18 to integration, partnership, boundary busting and greater interaction and interdependence. There was a realization that they were now in a much more competitive market-place and that their best chance of competing in it lay in cooperating rather than competing with each other. There was a new realism about the need to present a united front to their three business customers. A number of main strands of action were agreed in order to begin to make this happen.

First, a broad structure for the new team was to be implemented. Apart from having a coordinating group that would span the different locations, it would organize most of its resources not according to traditional specialist disciplines, nor according to locations. The agreed mechanism for grouping people was that of 'themes'—broad areas of environmental problems that required the input of very many different disciplines in whichever location those happened to be found. The important thing about these is that they describe issues defined by their business clients as opposed to technologies or single specialisms, thus signalling an important change in emphasis. 'Theme-based and issue-driven' became the new way of working to capture this new approach. The themes were evolved and brought into line with the priorities within BP's overall HSE strategy. Themes include, for example, emergency response and crisis management, pollution prevention, waste management, noise and training/awareness. In addition, contacts local to clients were subsequently agreed. Each individual technologist then became a member of at least one, and frequently several, 'themes'.

Second, a mission statement was agreed that became one element of a communication process aimed, on the one hand, at securing the commitment of senior management at each of the three main locations and, on the other hand, explaining the concept to all the HSE technologists. It also initiated the process of 'marketing' the new service to the businesses. A standard set of presentation slides became the vehicle for different people to convey a consistent message in presentations given by different members of the team over the following few months in Brussels, Lisbon, Cleveland, Aberdeen and London.

The third outcome was simply a commitment to have more contacts. Joint visits into the businesses were arranged; the transatlantic telephone lines hummed. One of the theme areas looking at issues relating to ground water and soil problems held a monthly videoconference across the Atlantic with an open agenda to share information and discuss issues and opportunities. Other groups, too, started to use the videoconferencing facilities on a much more regular basis.

A fourth, though later, outcome was that the three main locations submitted a jointly developed R&D programme to be funded by the businesses for the first time—an important achievement and symbol for the team and an important signal to the corporation.

Skills awareness

The fifth element of the implementation plan had been highlighted by four major issues that recurred repeatedly throughout the workshop:

1 people in general did not know what resources and skills were available at other locations
2 people did not reveal what they knew for various reasons, with the result that stereotypes continued to exist about which locations had which expertise
3 clients wanted one-stop shopping—they did not want to have the job of finding the best expertise and coordinating it—so the team needed some mechanism by which people with the relevant expertise for a client's specific problem could be identified
4 because in some areas people did not know their counterparts, there was not as much sharing of learning and best practice throughout the locations as was desired, so opportunities for cross-fertilization of ideas and spreading best practice were being lost.

A member of the team, based in Uxbridge, was asked to take on responsibility for developing a solution to these problems on behalf of the whole team.

He was introduced to a software company working on the development of a new approach to analysing, recording and disseminating the skills and expertise of individuals within organizations. They were looking for 'Beta test sites', software jargon for clients who would act as guinea pigs for testing the first working prototypes of a software system. This proposition suited the International HSE team's situation very well and a development agreement was struck whereby they would cooperate in the development of the prototype system to cover 80–100 people over the three locations.

The expertise database

The approach, based on an 'electronic questionnaire disk', was tailored to the needs of the HSE Technology Team in terms of the structure of questions on it. These were designed to help people record their experience and expertise in a very systematic manner. A particularly important element of this tailoring of the disk was ensuring that people 'filling in' the questionnaire could relate to it easily, it contained examples that were relevant to help them in doing their entries and it was made as easy as possible for them to fill in. So, for example, it gave lists of many company-specific examples that they had to tick rather than having to remember many details themselves. On average, it was estimated that each individual took about three hours to input the data about their past experience. The HSE Technology Team considered this investment of time to be more than justified in terms of the subsequent capabilities that the resulting database provided to all locations.

The resulting data on available expertise then enabled the team to start to compare what demands were being made by businesses (identified in the discussions with them on issues and the subsequent mapping of these into themes) with the actual supply of skills and experience within the themes. Through this ongoing process, the database will help them with their long-term resource planning and customer responsiveness.

Gaining commitment

An implementation issue was how to ensure that individuals were honest with themselves and others about their expertise. It was finally agreed that theme leaders would be able to see and discuss individual's data with them where they felt there were possibly distortions or inaccuracies.

This discussion process revealed the extra potential of the system as a personal development tool. Many individuals reported that they found filling it in to be thought provoking and stimulating as it got them to look comprehensively at their skills 'tool kit' for the first time and thus also highlighted some gaps.

The questions were tested out first on a few individuals, then amended, then tested again on a small group of nine people to get feedback about whether the kind of information that needed to be collected was being comprehensively dealt with in the questions. The overall concept of the database, the successive development versions of the electronic questionnaire and the system for retrieving relevant information from the database, were repeatedly demonstrated and described to many different key players. They all needed to back the concept and feel confident in the quality and usefulness of the information it would provide. There were some, too, who needed to be assured that the system was not duplicating related initiatives underway in other parts of the group. This iterative development process was important in gaining widespread acceptance of the system.

Other issues also had to be explored, such as whether the data would be held on two or three PCs in each of the four sites and accessed by people there or whether all the information about people's skills should be available on an open network that could be accessed from all locations. The team agreed that, initially, there would be one or two retrieval systems on PCs at each major site, but that the long-term ideal was for it to be openly accessible on a network or even on a videotex system linked directly to the businesses.

During the later stages of development, the skills database was introduced to the client businesses as part of the HSE Technology Team's marketing efforts. Clients were able to search early pilot versions of the database and get immediate, visible information about the range and depth of HSE skills on offer.

In time, it is hoped that the database will be extended to include specialists based in many more different locations around the world. The team estimates that there might be up to 500 other HSE-related professionals and interested parties within the BP group who would benefit from having their own expertise recorded on the database and being able to find out about that of others. Another participant observed, 'it's very good to be able to advertise myself . . . the first information step in stimulating exchange through networking'.

Conclusion

The International HSE Technology Team story within BP illustrates a number of important lessons. First, such cross-location, cross-country teams and their associated widespread networks of related specialists will become increasingly common. Second, history creates boundaries that prevent teamworking and those do not just dissolve by themselves; you have to design processes of team development to do this. Third, these dispersed groups need multiple mechanisms in order to communicate with each other. Fourth, both the team members and their clients must have high-quality mechanisms that enable them to make visible, and therefore fully to capitalize on, the skills iceberg that resides within the organization.

Human skill is the limiting factor. Access to skill is becoming more important than ownership. The acid test of organization is whether it can harness the talents of people wherever they or to whomever they 'belong'.[1]

Colin Coulson-Thomas, British author and consultant

In the computer world, we talk about the computer screen being WYSIWYG (pronounced wizzywig and standing for what you see is what you get). In the future the organization 'screen' will have to be WYSIWWL (wizzywill . . . what you see is what we've learned).[2]

1   Know-how as an asset

One of the unwitting results of the flatter hierarchy is that nobody knows any longer what people in other departments actually do. There are no functional middle managers to act as the bridge for communications. So, even if one specialist wants to be a good teamworker and elicit contributions from others, it is difficult to know where to start looking. This is particularly acute in organizations where informal contacts directly across functions have, in the past, been frowned upon and a networking culture has yet to take root. As organizations grow and where operations start to spread across many locations in many countries, it becomes impossible for *everyone* to know *all* the people with relevant expertise. This is exacerbated by constant change as cutbacks and mergers constantly shift the organization map.

Companies are beginning to ask fundamental questions about how they can codify such people's know-how so that it can be communicated, further developed and provide added value. If people leave the organization, how do you retain the know-how that they have built up within it? If you have skilled people in one location, how do you transmit or move their know-how to other locations where it is required? If you hire new people, how are their skills advertised? This mobility of knowledge, particularly in multinationals, is of fundamental importance.

There is also another philosophical and practical question as to just how much of an individual's experience and expertise is actually drawn upon by organizations. Individuals frequently answer this question by saying, 'in practice, not as much as they could'. The organization, therefore, only benefits from the visible top of the know-how iceberg. If managers actually mean it when they say, 'people are our greatest asset' and 'in the future it's our knowledge that we will be selling', then there should be many around who are seriously concerned about the poor return and utilization level that they are achieving from this knowledge asset lying invisible and underutilized in people's heads. Maximizing the return on an organization's know-how investment will be the most significant source of competitive edge in the future. The New Organization is all about finding new approaches to attracting, unearthing, developing, sharing and retaining know-how.

Semantics

Before exploring answers to these points, let me take a brief detour into semantics. I shall be using words such as 'knowledge', 'know-how', 'skill', 'expertise' and 'experience' interchangeably. For the pedantic, this area is a delight, but in organizations it can be a minefield because many of these words are used to mean different things by different people. I take all of these words to encompass things people know about, things they know how to do and the knowledge they have about what is likely to work in what circumstances. I also take them to mean the understanding people develop of why things work in a particular way and, therefore, how they can be reproduced in other settings, as well as the factual knowledge that they have both of things and people. Equally important nowadays, too, is a different kind of know-how—knowing what you do not know. This, in turn, triggers yet another kind of know-how, that to do with exploration, creativity, problem solving and so on which enables you to find answers to problems. In addition, each individual has the ability to acquire new know-how, new skills and new insights into how the world works, what can be achieved and how to achieve it. The process by which these new capabilities are acquired are frequently referred to as either learning or development. All of this, for me, is encapsulated by words such as knowledge, experience, expertise, skill and know-how.

Stocktaking

Demographic changes are making it increasingly difficult for organizations to find the quality of people they require. A report into the human resource requirements in the City in London[3] (the financial sector, an area of work which is heavily knowledge-based) was very critical of companies for their attitudes towards attracting and developing know-how. Particularly following the deregulation of the City, there was a huge expansion in services and a shortage of skilled people to provide them. The basic strategy of most organizations was, and still is, to poach talent from one another by driving salaries higher and higher. The concern of the report entitled 'Create or Abdicate', was that if this trend were to continue, the City would simply price itself out of the international market for financial services and would not be adding in any way to its knowledge capital. Few of these financial institutions had given thought to other ways in which they might attract, retain, develop and add value to their people.

How *do* we go about putting value on knowledge capital? If know-how is a key asset, where does it appear on the balance sheet? If there was a way of measuring both individuals' and organizations' know-how, it would make some of the purposes and outcomes of networking easier to track. Organizations do this in very partial ways, by taking head counts of those filing patents and trademarks, taking out copyrights and registering intellectual property, but, still, this whole field is in its infancy.

How different it would be if know-how did indeed appear on the balance sheet. How different then would organizations' attitudes be towards making people redundant and acquiring and attracting new people if their balance sheets were affected. How different would their attitudes be to training and development if it affected their share price. How differently they might then view older people with their particular kinds of experience and wisdom. How differently a company's approach to investment decisions might be if it was thinking in terms of developing its corporate knowledge base. How the perceived worth and role of Human Resource Development people might change if 'know-how value' or 'return on knowledge employed' became one of the company's main performance measures. How the difficult process of valuing service companies (with few tangible assets) involved in acquisitions might be improved. Such approaches to valuation might also make it easier for organizations to audit and map the know-how they have. If know-how is such a key commodity, then its assessment and development should be a key part of the strategic thinking of all organizations.

The know-how iceberg

Yves Doz, an impressive thinker and researcher from INSEAD, the business school outside Paris, points out that, particularly for international organizations, the ability to acquire and make knowledge mobile is a key factor. He goes on to say, 'the role of the acquisition and development of unique non-tradable assets (i.e., knowledge) is the key factor that differentiates companies that successfully achieve a strategy versus those that do not succeed in achieving the same strategy'.[4]

Most of these assets are not measured and remain invisible within the organization. In one sense, the invisible part is because the *people* are 'invisible'. In another sense, though, it is because the people's expertise is not always made visible to other people; they hide their light under a bushel. In addition, there is a category of expertise that the individual has but is not necessarily aware of or does not necessarily value. This can sometimes be visible to other people, but is not always so. Individuals need to know how to identify and access their *own* experience and expertise in all dimensions, but also need to be able to access the expertise of other people within the organization. More and more, too, they also need to know how to access relevant expertise outside the organization.

So how do we record, measure and value this elusive commodity? How do we release it from within people's heads if it is lying there dormant, forgotten or simply never called upon? How do others access that information or how is it to be shared so as to make it available to those who need it in a form that can be easily understood and is useful? How, then, can people in organizations add value to that know-how as they learn from each other? How can the organization keep track of and measure its stock of this shifting resource? In short, how do we make knowledge a mobile, valued asset within the New Organization?

These are not solely problems for large organizations with people in different locations or countries. Rapid knowledge diffusion and mobility is one of the attractions of a small organization, but organizations even as small as 60 or 70 people begin to find that their size mitigates against the kind of exchange, sharing and learning from each other that small companies enjoy. Even in organizations of this relatively small size, they find that they no longer know what everybody does.

Limiting factors

The way in which people find out about the expertise of colleagues inside and outside their organizations is a random process that depends on the work they happen to have done and the contacts they have thus acquired through their working careers. It is also very dependent on the *nature* of the work they have done and whether it brings them into contact with other people to any great extent. It is also partly dependent on the personality of the individuals concerned and their degree of inquisitiveness and interest in other people. Some people take to it more naturally then others. For the individual, of course, there is a real Catch 22. As one project leader put it to me, 'the trouble is I don't know who I don't know and I don't know what I need to know that I don't already know'.

Informal networks address the mapping and access question to some extent, but they only go so far. The problem is that you only know the people you know. Your contacts diminish outside your own functional area, decay and are not renewed. Hidden areas of a person's expertise are often never uncovered and what is relevant knowledge changes over time.

Another limiting factor comes from people's own perceptions of their expertise, experience and self-worth. I have already referred elsewhere to the sense of identity that many people find in professional expertise and membership and the sense of loss they experience when they feel that this is being stripped away in the more fluid multifunctional organization. People who have acquired some kind of specialist expertise tend to define the whole of their experience in such terms. If we go to a party and ask the standard question of another guest, 'What do you do?' the response tends to be, 'I am a truck driver', 'I am an accountant', 'I am a managing director' or whatever. These responses show a very narrow way of thinking. People seldom describe themselves in terms of the competences they have acquired in their social or leisure lives, such as the secretary who sits on the board of governors of a school, the accountant who runs the local amateur dramatics society or the truck driver who has a handicapped child and is heavily involved in a society for handicapped children. Even within the context of a specific discipline, I have frequently been startled by the number of times people say things like, 'Oh, nobody else will be interested in that' or 'No, that was just a one-off, unique situation. It's not relevant to anything else that anybody else does.'

How wrong these people are. We know well from studies of innovations and breakthroughs,[5] that it is just this combining together of know-how from disparate and unconventional sources that is the well-spring for significant leaps forward. If you talk to consultants involved in outplacement activities or in vocational counselling for people in mid career, they will say that a key battle is to get their clients to define their experience in a much wider way, to value the competences that they have acquired across the whole range of their activities and to see these as assets that they can then utilize in very different environments in the future. It is this kind of reframing that people who have been made redundant need to do to give new value to their lives by realizing the many other ways in which they can contribute. Organizations must begin to help all their people to reframe and value their expertise more broadly.

One such approach is used by Merck, the major US pharmaceutical company, voted repeatedly by the readers of *Fortune* as America's most admired company. It provides its people with the opportunity to go through a wide range of personal assessments, using a variety of methods, such as psychological inventories, in-tray exercises and simulations. The aim is to encourage people to learn much more about themselves and their capabilities. The Leadership Development Program, pioneered by the Center for Creative Leadership in Greensboro, North Carolina, and now licensed to other institutions world-wide, puts people through an intensive and rewarding process of self, peer and objective feedback that provides a similar detailed stocktake of one's wider skills and attributes.

2   Making the invisible, visible

Codifying people's experience

The goal of a comprehensive database providing easy access to detailed information on people's knowledge and experience is still a tantalizing goal to go for, as Lynda Applegate and her colleagues at the Harvard Business School predict in their survey of the future of IT. 'Computers will also help identify who in the company has the expertise needed to work on a particular problem. Databases of employee's skills and backgrounds will ensure that the mix of talent can be tailor-made for every task that arises. The systems will keep track of who knows what, and how to prepare an individual for the next project.'[6]

The practical applications

Suppose we could find a way to make this hidden expertise available on tap. There would be a number of operational benefits. For example, it would enable the organization to pull together project teams or clusters in a way that effectively took account of the different contributions that individuals would be likely to make. Project teams, as we have seen, are formed for all kinds of reasons: major contracts, investment analysis, strategic planning, new product development, policy reviews and so on. These teams are increasingly sourced from throughout the organization rather than from individual parts of it. The more complicated and the bigger the organization, the more difficult it is to find and bring together the best people. The potential result may be that major projects are delayed, with possibly quite serious financial and other penalties, the best teams are not formed, leading to lower quality of project delivery and lower morale, and key opportunities are missed when people with relevant information are not identified. It would also enable salespeople to identify internal experts rapidly and comprehensively so that they could be matched, as individuals, to clients' problems. It would also ensure that the organization managed its clients (internal or external) in an integrated fashion, taking advantage of the fact that several of its staff or units may, at any time, be interacting with the same client.

Such a system would also have a number of strategic benefits. It would allow the organization, for example, to increase the rate of know-how exchange between its people and so help the organization to learn by building of human networks, supported by the computer, that erode internal boundaries. It could also help ensure that senior management were staying very sensitive to what was happening externally. It could identify weak signals from the environment that could be transmitted by those individuals most in touch with it. Above all, however, such a system would hold out the prospect of the organization truly understanding what know-how it had (and what it didn't have and had to acquire). It could, for the first time, begin to audit and put value on its knowledge base in a more systematic way. This would have important implications, for example, were the organization was the target of a takeover bid or where its investment in people may not be fully reflected in the share price. Programmes or projects may be seriously delayed when newly appointed managers have to invest time learning about their staff, and gaps in future skill requirements may not be identified early enough, thus meaning that the organization is unable to respond to important opportunities.

The traditional method

For organizations who have sensed the needs above, two kinds of response have been available. The traditional response would be to rely on induction processes and informal networking, coupled with the production of an internal telephone directory and perhaps a newsletter. A more ambitious approach would be to fill out questionnaires and attempt to set up an in-house paper-based directory of who does what. This might then be transferred to a computerized database. The induction and informal networking approach, however, has severe limitations in times of rapid technical change or when the organization is reshaping itself. The same is true when organizations are growing rapidly in terms of numbers and locations. Informal networks and static information sources tend to lag behind.

A computerized database, on the other hand, is potentially dynamic. Growth and change are things it can cope with. The problem here, as those who have tried it can testify, is that the reality of computerized expertise databases falls short of the promise.

It is easy for organizations to underestimate the sheer costs and administrative burden that have to be supported year after year. A questionnaire has to be thought through, printed, sent out, followed up (because nobody likes filling in forms), returned edited, input, sent back for checking and then input onto a database. Then the whole process has to be repeated every 6 to 12 months. New skills necessary for creating a database have to be learned. For example, if the database is to be searchable, it has to be edited. This requires knowledge of editing rules and editors. Computing skills are necessary to design and manage the database. Liaison and administration is required and so on. If the scale of the operation is small or the skills are outside the organization's mainstream area, the task can be seen as a distraction.

More fundamentally, perhaps, there may also be a mismatch between the whole questionnaire approach and the task it has to do. Besides the fact that questionnaires are static forms trying to capture data that changes frequently, there is also the problem of the depressant effect they have on the quality of data being captured. They are tedious. Like the iceberg, nine tenths of anyone's expertise tends to be hidden below the surface and has to be drawn out. 'Another questionnaire' does not stimulate people to produce the required information.

Box 7.1   Do not re-invent the wheel

A large practice of international lawyers with offices throughout the world found out by accident that partners taking on new cases were sometimes repeating work that had been done by other people on other cases in other places and at other times. They decided that this process of re-inventing the wheel was extremely inefficient and if they could find a way of being able to identify where similar work had been done beforehand, that this would give them a significant competitive advantage.

By a process of trial and error, they developed a database to help them do this. What they had thought would be a simple undertaking turned out to be highly complicated and much more difficult than they had ever imagined, involving considerable time and money on the part of different people. Also eliciting relevant and useful information from the database was time-consuming and highly technical and, even then, the answers were frequently out of date. The database gradually died of neglect and lack of use.

Some very innovative research and development work has been done at 3E

Research, a software company based in Scotland. They have acquired unique experience in building expertise databases while recording research going on in UK universities in order to market it round the world. Now they have come up with a simple but radical approach that promises a way forward within organizations. Having seen the problems, they are aware that a new approach is necessary if organizations are to introduce successful in-house systems. It comes in the form of an approach called XXEN (pronounced 'zen').

Design principles

XXEN has had to incorporate a number of principles. The administrative burden of the system must be minimal. The system must run itself. This means that there must be no editing, data input, system design and so on. Almost everything must be computerized. The 3E system collects data not on paper questionnaires, but on floppy disks via an electronic questionnaire using a mixture of structured and unstructured questions. The computer, in effect, 'interviews' individuals and enables them to enter ordinary text and description. Software on the disk edits the data and converts it into a form suitable for instant loading into a pre-designed information management and retrieval system.

The second principle is that the quality of the data entered must be high; people must be encouraged to reveal the nine tenths of their iceberg, which is achieved by using prompts to draw people out. There is also a strong emphasis on making the process enjoyable (if it is not, no one will invest their time in entering their data). This is achieved by using humour and graphic design as important elements and by advising people on how to prepare themselves for the process.

Once people's experience and expertise is recorded, then that expertise must be made available to everyone who needs it. It is no good having information that can only be acquired by going up and down the organization chart. It is also no good having data that only experts can retrieve. XXEN is designed to be searched by *anyone* and it creates a database that can be put on a PC, be part of a network or be accessed on-line. Questions that searchers could ask of it might include, for example:

- 'We want to put together a new project team to work on optical sensors in our German subsidiary. Who are our experts? Who can speak German? Has anyone worked in Germany before?'
- 'I am Chief Executive of my Group. I want to know what has happened to the collective know-how of my company over the last five years. I know profits have been rising, but have we run down our know-how base?'
- 'We believe that object-orientated programming is going to be important in the next five years. What is the age profile of our experts? Do we have enough? Should we be recruiting more?'

- 'I am new to this company and need to know which of my colleagues have things I need. Moreover, I want them to know what I can do.'

Apple is also developing a special form of computer network called Spider,[7] which is designed to tell a manager instantly whether an employee is available to join a project, what the employee's skills are and where the employee is located. Motorola and others have done similar things, too. These solutions, however, are tailor-made for one organization. The challenge here (which seems to have been addressed by 3E Research), is to develop a generic system that can learn as it goes along and be applied equally, with appropriate tailoring, to every kind of organization. As this new approach develops, by the new millennium we should understand a lot more about melting icebergs and making know-how mobile than we do at the moment.

3   Themes and programmes

Another important strategy for nurturing knowledge is the increasing use of knowledge 'themes' and 'programmes' throughout and outside the organization. These serve to focus and make visible the range of company's know-how in a particular area and, in so doing, make it easier to quantify, audit and value. If the stock can be seen, it can, at least, be counted—if only in terms of the number of people involved.

Themes and programmes serve an important function in providing individuals with identity within the network. Whereas within traditional organizations, identity was created by means of professional specialisms or organizational units, the network, apart from clustering people together to achieve specific projects, will also create larger clusters around broad problem areas, usually defined from a client perspective. For example, the BP's HSE Technology Team is a focused network within the wider BP network that is broadly concerned to help solve its customers' environmental problems. The Healthy Cities multicity action programmes on topics such as AIDS and tobacco provide focus, yet again, on a broad set of problems and issues. In research and development organizations, they are increasingly talking about research *programmes*, not only research projects.

The idea of a programme is particularly useful where the overall goals and targets are too uncertain to be easily converted into specific project outputs. A programme may also be concerned with a broader range of activities over a much longer timescale where the goals will evolve and change both in terms of external demands and regarding new techniques or methods within the area. A programme, like a theme, draws together and makes visible an organization's know-how about certain categories and problems.

Corian Sasse,[8] a Dutch consultant, provides some good examples of the differences between programmes and projects that are summarized in Box 7.2.

Box 7.2   Programmes vs. projects

Programme	Project
• the conception, development and introduction of a new product line	• the development and introduction of a specified product
• the development of environmentally sound methods of shore protection	• measuring the release of toxic components of certain materials used in shore protection
• introducing and implementing project management in the organization	• writing a handbook for project managers
• researching uses of alternative energy sources	• study of the feasibility of using wind turbines for local electricity networks

These themes or programmes do provide another way of branding a network. Indeed, both in the case of BP and WHO, there was considerable debate over the name to be given to the themes and programmes—a very clear clue as to the importance of the identity that these were providing. One thing must be said, however, which is that themes and programmes are not simply the reinvention of functions or specialisms, nor are they simply a new version of the matrix organization. Themes and programmes, and the people who identify with them, are essentially multidisciplinary in nature. They are vehicles for addressing complicated problems that cross traditional functional boundaries.

They are also vehicles for drawing together and focusing a wide range both of formal projects, routine day-to-day activity, the management of interfaces and connections between these different activities and what Sasse calls 'improvisations'—a way of expressing the fact that not all programme or theme activity is planned in advance. By its very dynamic nature, there will be unexpected opportunities and demands, creative new possibilities that emerge out of the blue and which are very important to the dynamic development of the programme.

References

1 Coulson-Thomas, Colin (1990) 'The Responsive Organisation', *Journal of General Management*, Vol. 15, No. 4, Summer.
2 This idea emerged while talking to a group of software specialists about how they could find out about each others' skills.
3 Rajan, Amin and Julie Fryatt (1988) *Create or Abdicate: The City's Human Resource Choice for the 90s*, Witherby & Co, London.
4 Doz, Yves (1989) 'Knowledge as a corporate Asset', presentation to European Forum for Management Development Research Conference, Barcelona, April.
5 Nayak, Ranganath and John Ketteringham (1986) *Breakthroughs*, Mercury Books, London.
6 Copyright © (1988) of the President and Fellows of Harvard College; all rights reserved. Reprinted by permission of *Harvard Business Review*. Lynda Applegate, James Cash and D Quinn Mills (1988) 'Information Technology and Tomorrow's Manager', *Harvard Business Review*, November-December, pp 128–136.
7 Dumaine, Brian (1991), 'The Bureaucracy Busters', *Fortune*, 17 June, pp 36–50.
8 Sasse, Corian (1992) 'Management by Programs: a new focus', in Proceedings of 11th Internet World Congress on Project Management, Florence (Project Management Without Boundaries), Edizioni Unicopli, Milan.

Pictures in the mind

The organiscope

We have all seen computer graphics on television—images suddenly break up, fragment, rotate, change colour and, perhaps, then re-form into a different shape or from a different perspective. Some people may be familiar with Computer Aided Design (CAD) software that can draw three-dimensional images on the screen and then enable the viewer to look at those images from different angles, both inside and outside the object. There is some even more remarkable software that can design extraordinarily complicated shapes with twisting tunnels and routes within it in a kaleidoscopic fantasy of colour. IBM even employ a sculptor to help create these wonderful visualizations.

Given this remarkable graphic computing power, would it not be possible to go way beyond the sterility and two-dimensional nature of the traditional organigram.

My fantasy is that we could represent the organization visually in many dimensions, using the power of design, movement and colour to describe different aspects of the organization. The picture I have is of someone journeying through the organization as a space ship might travel through the galaxy. As we looked out of the window we would see different elements of the organization, individuals, departments and locations, as well as information about the different ways in which they were connected to each other. We would see where expertise was located. We would 'meet' people in different locations.

The organiscope would then be a powerful tool for new people trying to find their feet in the New Organization, as well as helping external people find the right contacts.

Everyone could 'see' in summary the different kinds of work going on. It could also represent the dynamic and changing nature of the organization over time.

Science fiction or reality just round the corner? We shall see.

8
Hard networks—how to realize the potential of new communications technology

PATHFINDER
Benetton

To many consumers, the fashion industry symbolizes glamour, the smart set and a life of luxury. What many of them will not be aware of is that behind this media façade lies an industry facing some of the toughest challenges and pressures in business today. As a matter of sheer survival, fashion has taken a lead in discovering how to deal with radical new problems and issues.

By its very nature, the fashion industry is an international one where the constant search for new ideas and trends creates a degree of volatility and a need for responsiveness that is quite without parallel. While Paris, Milan, Tokyo and London are seen as the heart of the exclusive world of *haute couture*, it is the mass fashion business that operates on a truly global scale. There is no company that symbolizes this better than Italy's Benetton, which has come to epitomize the renaissance of Italian fashion around the world.

Benetton has built a dynamic international fashion empire, now operating in 100 countries throughout the world. It has become a household name by virtue of its large number of stores, its controversial international advertising campaigns and its many sponsorships, notably of Formula One racing cars. The roots of this international enterprise lie in the Veneto region of Northern Italy, an area noted for the resourcefulness and industriousness of its people.

While the company is certainly global, its whole way of operating is based on the realization that its customers are not. It seeks to put into practice a degree of product customization that would be the envy of any manufacturer. It is based on a highly developed customer-led philosophy of targeted marketing. At the same time, Benetton seeks to preserve the economies of scale so vital to success in a highly competitive industry. It achieves both in its very structure and innovative use of IT.

The elements of the network

Benetton's building blocks are its, approximately, 7000 stores around the world. Each of these is run as a totally separate business, owned and managed by an independent storeowner. These entrepreneur shopowners choose to invest significant sums of capital, which they raise, in starting up a Benetton store. They become autonomous businesses that undertake to buy an agreed minimum quantity of merchandise, which they select from the approximately 7500 items in the two extensive annual Benetton collections. They also undertake to feed back to Benetton specified market and financial information.

Benetton is driven by an entrepreneural distribution culture and the way it finds and selects its storeowners is central to the implementation of this culture. They are recruited by an exclusive group of 80 representatives, who seek out hungry young entrepreneurs whose *modus operandi* is compatible with Benetton's philosophy. These representatives were originally all Italian, but now are of other nationalities as well. They are frequently people who have owned or do own their own stores and they form a trusted, influential group within the inner circle of Benetton. They, in turn, are all self-employed and work on a commission basis. Their job is to scan their particular territory, find locations for new stores, screen sites, identify potential new storeowners, communicate orders and market trends to the centre and introduce the new fashion collections to the individual stores within a particular territory. Many of them have become millionaires in their own right. The combination of these entrepreneurial roles forms a highly motivated group that is the distribution powerhouse of Benetton.

At the other end of the supply chain, Benetton takes this same entrepreneural philosophy and implements it in a similar, though not identical, manner. There are 5500 employees who work directly for Benetton in Europe and North and South America. In addition to these, a network of subcontractors substantially increases the company's access to manpower—25000 people work for Benetton subcontractors in Italy alone. This same model is reproduced in all the countries in which Benetton has manufacturing facilities: Argentina, Brazil, France, Spain and the US. Licensing agreements and joint ventures extend the involvement of subcontractors even further. Among the most recent of the latter have been joint ventures set up in the rapidly developing markets of India, Egypt, Turkey and Poland.

The Italian core of this network of subcontractors reflects the pattern of the fashion industry in Italy. Italy's textile industry has long been dominated by medium-sized, family-owned enterprises, located in well-defined regions. People know each other personally and have built up close-knit patterns of interdependent relationships over the years, a phenomenon also typical of other industrial sectors in Italy.

For Benetton, the sharing of manufacturing responsibility (by means of the networks of subcontractors) results in greater industrial efficiency for both parties. Benetton can spread the risk of its production liabilities, yet retain a degree of flexibility and responsiveness that large production units would find it difficult to match. The subcontractors also benefit; they have more autonomy and individual responsibility. Both parties gain by achieving increased efficiency, supporting investment in new technology and the transfer of 'best business practice' among members of the network

Soft and hard networks

The job of orchestrating the efforts of both its production and distribution subcontractors is carried out from Benetton's headquarters in Veneto. On the same site it has collected together those core functions that it feels cannot be subcontracted externally because they are either capital-intensive, are central to the quality of the product or provide the basic communications infrastructure of the organization. Centralized production processes are limited to design, wool processing, dying, technological research, cutting and quality control.

These core production processes are linked to the activities of production subcontractors by means of a sophisticated electronic communications network, an automated warehouse and computerization of key manufacturing tasks, such as knitting machines and fabric cutters, that have been built up slowly and systematically by Veneto over the last few years.

Initially Benetton's expansion was based on a number of factors other than electronic communications. Personal relationships were important and, in particular, the network formed by senior management and the representatives. So, too, was modernization of its production plant and the approach to store and product design. However, Benetton quickly began to realize the enormous benefits in terms of responsiveness and efficiency that an integrated approach to IT and data exchange could bring. An increasingly sophisticated IT system was introduced, which started with computerized design and cutting processes and then spread to warehousing, shipping, production and back into day-to-day stock control and sales. EDI (electronic data interchange) is used to transmit data on sales and stock trends 24 hours a day.

In addition to automating the overall production cycle, Benetton also utilized IT to connect its headquarters with its far-flung network of representatives world-wide. By means of such automation and connectability, Benetton was able to create a situation where it was possible to deliver an order of a specific item from the collection to a store within three days of the the representative's order. Using IT, it also became possible to design and manufacture so-called 'flash' products—new ideas or niches not reflected in the more pre-planned collections—and to do so in less than three months from concept to delivery. This degree of speed and responsiveness is the envy of many manufacturers, not only in the fashion industry. In effect, the IT system has the effect of linking the shop, via the representative, directly to the factory floor, the designer, via the representative, directly to the customer, the automated warehouse directly to the supplier and the store and all the stores, via the representatives, directly to the financial and market nerve centre at Benetton's headquarters.

The other function to be coordinated from the centre is the overall corporate planning process in which many of the representatives and storeowners become involved. For example, the company's two major annual collections are shown to representatives before going into production.

Culture and style

There is no doubt that the Benetton style grows directly out of an Italian approach to business and relationships. Most storeowners have no formal contract with the company. Relationships are based on trust between the representatives and the people they recruit and on a sense of shared responsibility, support and 'family feeling'. In most cases, this culture has been successfully conveyed and exported by the representatives to other countries.

The one country in which there have been some problems as a culture clash emerged, is the USA, interestingly enough. Many US storeowners wanted a formal relationship with a more contractual and legal, rather than social and informal, approach. In many parts of the world, representatives will open up Benetton stores very close to each other, often on the same street where they find the increased visibility brings greater business, particularly as the range of products grows. Some individual storeowners wanted much larger, defined and exclusive territories and catchment areas. After some time, Benetton adapted its way of operating in the US to encompass these expectations.

Another important part of the Benetton culture is the emphasis on travel by senior managers and representatives. A strong element in the corporate ethos is that all the key people should be in continuous contact with different markets around the world to develop a feel for them through hands-on experience. They should exchange notes and ideas, taking what works in one market and applying it in another. This passion for travel is another very tangible way in which Benetton's 'globalization' (think global, act local) is put into practice.

As another tangible element in its constant search for ideas and innovation, Benetton brings designers to Italy from all over the world. That alone guarantees a fertile combination of ideas, but the added spice is that these designers, by and large, only come in for two or three years maximum and are then replaced by new ones in order to keep ideas constantly flowing. Constant inward mobility of this nature keeps Benetton closely in touch with shifting fashion trends and changing consumer tastes.

Issues

The extent to which Benetton is, in fact, a networking organization may be subject to question. For, while it is highly decentralized in an organizational sense, there does not appear to be a significant devolution of power. Clearly, in electronic terms, it is highly networked, but the electronic communication mechanisms serve primarily to relay information between the centre and the periphery and back again rather than foster direct communication between shops or between different subcontractors.

Another issue is whether the progressive introduction of new management methods and further technologies will compromise Benetton's original culture of trust and informality. It has been suggested that the company could suffer the usual fate of the classic, family-owned business in Italy once members of the founding family retire. It is often said in the fashion industry that brands begin as the passion of one person and lose their way when that person is gone. Luciano Benetton has stated that 'successful brands are those able to substitute the cult of personality with a more generic and communicable set of values through networks'. The early introduction of 'outside' managers since the seventies will, it is hoped, ensure a smooth transition.

Nevertheless, in its radically decentralized organization structure, its sophisticated use of communications technologies, the important role of its core network of representatives who carry, pass on and sustain the Benetton way of doing things, its long-term partnerships based on trust with a 'family' of small suppliers and its senior executives' commitment to travel, illustrates how the elements of the New Organization contribute not only to market responsiveness, but also to an enviable performance record during times of substantial organizational change. Its core networks, both hard and soft, are an important part of the success story.[1,2,3]

These are the vital things, things for which we have no answers:

- managing change that we can't see in advance, and caused by a technology that management doesn't understand
- rationalizing the role of the centre when the technology offers ever-increasing self-sufficiency to the individual
- creating automated systems whose total complexity is beyond our grasp
- justifying investment in a technology whose benefits we can't measure.

Kit Grindley, quoting Senior IT Executive[4]

Accessible, well-defined data and a transparent network are, therefore, the keys to effective integration in the coming years. Developing these resources, however, is not easy. Justifying organization-spanning networks whose benefits are uncertain and will occur in the future, and whose costs cannot be attributed clearly to any specific suborganization, is in part an act of faith. Developing common coding systems and data definitions is a herculean job. This task increases short-term costs for long-term gain—a practice not encouraged by most of today's measurement systems.

John Rockart and James Short, MIT Sloan School of Management[5]

1   Frustrated expectations

The potential

The world of electronic communications has captured the imagination of old and young alike. Its power has been brought home dramatically, particularly through the medium of television. There will be few people around the world who did not, at some point, see the dramatic events unfolding in Eastern Europe or in the Gulf War as they actually happened.

However, for most people working in organizations, the 1980s brought increasing exposure to some of the possibilities and pitfalls presented by the new communications technology. For many it may have started with the introduction of personal computers (PCs) and E-mail. Within these organizations, new terminologies such as 'computer conferencing', 'bulletin boards' or 'accessing external databases' sprung up. After a year or two, the E-mail system may have become available not only within a building, but also between sites and countries. Few people probably gave a second thought to the invisible system of cables, optical fibres and telecommunication satellites that enabled this electronic letter-writing to happen. Perhaps, at a subsequent stage, larger organizations started to advertise the availability of videoconferencing between sites. To many this seemed less convenient because you had to move away from your desk to a special studio in order to do it and you had to book a time for it to happen. However, at the same time, it presented the extraordinary sensation of being able to see one's colleagues talking at that moment in time, from another continent, to you!

While these may have been the main ingredients of the new technologies to which many office workers were exposed, those involved in engineering, design and manufacturing will have become aware of the technology in perhaps different ways. As in the Pathfinder story about Benetton, designers may have found themselves sitting in front of a computer aided design terminal experimenting with different shapes and colours for a garment. Once their design was finalized, it would be transmitted to another location and translated automatically into instructions either for the cutting of fabrics or for the selection and dyeing of different types of wool for a particular production run.

While the raw materials produced in this way were delivered to the production site automatically, instructions were also sent electronically to programme the knitting or sewing machines and to control the production flow. The resulting finished garments were then automatically tracked into an automated warehouse and stock picked based on information sent electronically from stores around the world. In this world, the networks consist of computers talking to each other.

It is perhaps significant that some of the most oft-quoted success stories in communications technology lie in the area of electronic data interchange—EDI. Bonney Stamper, an American EDI consultant, defines it as 'computer-to-computer exchange of business information in a standard data format'.[6] She describes how many companies, both large and small, realize benefits by being able to exchange information electronically. She goes on to say,

> Common business transactions that are accomplished through EDI are purchase orders, advanced shipping notices, invoices and many more. Using EDI for these types of transactions allows companies to do away with the tremendous amount of paper required with the 'traditional methods' companies have used for years. In addition, the speed of the exchange of information can be almost immediate with EDI versus the amount of time required when mailing documents and allowing for processing.[7]

These applications, as in the example of Benetton, require minimal human intervention. Indeed, many are totally automatic. Many of us as consumers are used to going through the supermarket checkout watching the product bar codes read by a laser reader. We see the price registered and our bill printed out automatically. What we do not see is how the EDI network updates the stockholding figure for each item while, at the end of the day, automatically sending to the warehouse a reorder that is automatically assembled with other items in a complete truckload. This is automatically delivered by the most cost-effective route for delivery at the time required by the local branch.

Disappointment

It is a cruel paradox that some of the greatest successes of electronic communications, much hyped by the IT world (aided and abetted by the media) have served to create the unrealistic belief that the communications and electronic data processing technologies can solve just about any problem. All parties, IT people, senior managers and users have had a part to play in this. The difference is that now senior managers and users are beginning to voice their frustrations and disappointments more openly. They say that many systems are driven by the technology and by what technology can do rather than by business *needs*. They say that many systems are overspecified, a consequence of this being that they feel huge amounts of money are being poured into projects that will never be fully utilized. They say that IT people are not sensitive enough to the impact of their technologies on the organization and on people, nor do they understand enough about the ways in which the technologies need to be developed to make then genuinely easy to use. They say that there are many unexpected organizational and human consequences of the technologies which they were not made aware of before investing in them. They say that IT people expect them to be clear about what they need and want, but fail to appreciate all the uncertainties, differing needs and objectives they are trying to juggle. They say that IT people are not always honest enough about the uncertainties and limitations of the technologies.

Such feelings of disappointment are now being complemented by more tangible research evidence that both comforts and shocks senior managers as they begin to realize that their companies are not alone in facing such problems with IT. One such piece of evidence comes from a survey conducted among 45 major companies in Austria on the success rate of major IT projects. Conducted by Roeland van Delzen, a Dutch IT consultant working in Austria, it revealed that 43 per cent of companies had experienced one or more major project failures in the past five years. Of these, 60 per cent (a quarter of the original sample) had experienced three or more major failures in the same time period.[8] What was disturbing was how many failed to *learn* from their experience. Roeland Van Delzen suggests that the failure rate might even be higher in reality as this data was obtained from IT specialists within the company, who might be expected to paint a rosier picture than non-technical colleagues. Box 8.1 illustrates the paradox of the possibilities and the day-to-day realities.

Box 8.1 Almost there, but not quite

Intel Chief sees rich data as key to PC's future

In the keynote address to the opening session of Comdex (the major US computer exhibition), Andrew S Grove, President and CEO of Intel Corporation, described his vision for the second decade of the PC. Rich Data—photographic-quality images, full-motion video and hi-fi quality sound—will be the currency of computing in the 90s, and the task of storing it and, crucially, moving it around between computers, will be the challenge facing the whole industry, both hardware and software-based. 'Business doesn't usually consist of people sitting quietly at PCs running spreadsheets', he told the packed Hilton Showroom audience, 'most office workers spend the majority of their days in meetings and conversations. Using tomorrow's PCs, we will confer via electronic mail with colleagues halfway round the world, working together to revise a document displayed on both our screens.' Technology, he said, would be in the background, collaborative problem solving in the foreground.

Achieving this aim would require major developments to improve the graphics capabilities of the PC, but Mr Grove was confident the technology was feasible. More critical, and less certain, was the degree of cooperation and compatibility which would be required between the suppliers and their products.

He drew a comparison between current PC networking offerings and the telephone system, saying that if the telephone had developed in the same way as PC networks, we'd need separate lines for personal and business calls, and an engineer to plug the phone into the wall socket. 'Computer-supported collaboration', he said, 'in which industry works together on common goals to improve work methods, must be our common goal.'

Then, to prove that things aren't really that bad today, he conducted a quite dazzling multivendor, multimedia display, which was marred only by a number of bent connectors on an expansion card and a flat battery on a cellular modem-equipped portable.

Almost there, but not quite.

PC Plus, December 1991, page 185[9]

2 Automation or transformation?

Diane Wilson, a researcher in the MIT Management for the 1990s programme, has carried out a detailed review of the different ways in which organizations evaluate the success of their IT investment.[10] Perhaps not surprisingly, she found a confused jungle of different, often conflicting success criteria put forward by different stakeholders.

What her study was able to highlight, however, was the dominant thought during the last 20 years that IT's fundamental role and purpose was the automation of current business systems. The automation model of the organization, the picture that many IT people hold in their minds, is still inherently that of a centralized, hierarchically and functionally divided bureaucracy. For many, their thinking is still heavily, perhaps unconsciously, dominated by the mainframe computer, which required the centralization and standardization of all information processes. The role of the central IT department was to exercise strong control over IT solutions. In this mind set, connectivity between different elements of the organization was very low and not of importance. Those same people also brought with them a mentality that required order, structure, logic and degrees of stability so that the large systems they were building would have a long life of payback and would need little alteration or amendment during that life.

Diane Wilson attributes part of the current confusion regarding measuring success to the rapidly growing alternative vision for IT, which sees the role and purpose of IT to be the *transformation* of organizational design and processes. However, as Alan Kamman of US consultants Nolan Norton observes, such a mind set is quite out of keeping with the new possibilities of decentralized computing opened up by PCs.

> The information infrastructure of the organization must be redesigned in conjunction with the business redesign. The processing of information will move out of the centralized paradigms associated with the hierarchical organizations of the past and into the distributed paradigms of the information era. Work stations and other distributed work platforms will dominate this environment: each work station will facilitate the added value of the knowledge worker, and all the work platforms will be linked by a network that promotes the dissemination of information throughout the organization.[11]

IT—a barrier to change?

Both IT agendas can, of course, coexist, but quite different approaches are needed and everyone gets muddled about what they are trying to achieve. For the transformers, the dream of the New Organization is at the root of the current role and purpose behind investment in IT. They can see ways in which IT, used radically, can produce a significant competitive advantage way beyond simply automating current processes. IT's role becomes central as an agent of change, facilitating the organization in doing things differently and not merely doing the same things better. However, the transformation mind set is held back in turn not only by the still-dominant automation mind set (and the technology associated with it), but also by the inadequacies of the newer technologies' ability to deliver the transformation agenda. Diane Wilson quotes one consultant who summarizes it well.

> We are up against a barrier today. We brought the technology in stand-alone islands of automation and we cannot move forward because we cannot integrate the pieces. Secondly, we cannot change the attitudes and the underlying processes that really open the door to big pay-offs.[12]

Standardization is not centralization

This situation has been created and maintained by the computer industry's continuing failure to establish simple standards to enable different types of systems to 'talk to each other'. Now the IT people will say that this is not necessary, that new standardized software protocols can enable different technologies and standards to be interconnected. Achieving this, however, introduces further complicated 'technologicalness' that takes access to it further and further away from ordinary users and pulls the power back more and more into the hands of the technical specialists.

Darrell Corbin, a systems analyst for Boeing in Seattle, was programme manager for Boeing Aerospace's international E-mail and videoconferencing system. He had the unenviable task of finding ways in which to link together many different parts of the organization, each of which was using different kinds of technology for E-mail. His conclusion was simple and blunt: 'The need for a company standard was mandatory.'[13] The result is continuing confusion in the IT mind set that believes necessary standardization requires centralization. They are not the same. The converse, however, is that the clients, the distributed users, have to reach agreement among themselves, with IT people unsure of their role in that process. So, until computers can talk to each other as effortlessly as telephones, we shall continue to live with ITs centralizing and automating tendencies, which lie uneasily alongside the transformation vision of the distributed organization.

The IT world thus finds itself caught literally and uncomfortably betwixt and between. It is at the transition point between the automation revolution and the transformation revolution, finding that the former is required less and less and the latter requires a very different role and approach for which many of them are ill equipped. Paradoxically, therefore, IT, seen once as the great warrior of change, suddenly finds itself branded as a *barrier* to change.

The senior management problem

Given the, at times, frustrated expectations of what the technology can currently do and the limitations that the more visionary managers often find of the IT mind set, many senior managers feel exposed and unhappy.

A book by Kit Grindley, Professor of Systems Automation at the London School of Economics, entitled *Managing IT at Board Level*,[14] puts the issues very succinctly. He interviewed senior executives in 102 corporations world-wide that had appointed IT directors. He points out that major companies recognize that they are totally dependent on their IT systems for day-to-day operations and that the correct strategic use of IT is vital for their future survival, but, at the same time, they find themselves frighteningly dependent on their IT experts. They make investment decisions that not only commit the company to spending huge amounts of money but, as with the arena of computer networking, may well govern the whole way that the company will run.

At this strategic level he points out that it is not the technology that makes the management of IT tough, it is that no one on the Board really supports the idea that the information network will be the company's most important asset in ten years' time. There is what Grindley calls a culture gap between IT executives, experts and the Boards that make it difficult for them to get along with each other. It is difficult for the senior team, for example, to be able to express their feelings of ignorance and, indeed, vulnerability in this crucial area. Many of them simply do not have the awareness and knowledge to make these extraordinarily complicated investment decisions. Where they are looking for answers and certainty, they see only uncertainty and cash going out of the door. What are they and the IT community to do about it?

3   Getting IT right

There are, of course, examples where IT is contributing to the transformation of organizations and doing so successfully, now. The issue is how to learn from these early successes and disseminate best practice. It is no solution to avoid developing hard network capability in the hope that, in the future, the soft networking technologies will be sufficient or that if the suppliers get the technology right, all will be well. There can be no doubt that those organizations that manage to find a way in which to get IT right—the technology installed and working, the people in the organization comfortable with it and enthusiastically using it and to support the power of soft networking—will gain significant competitive advantage. As the rate of success begins to increase, then the more disadvantaged will become those organizations that have not yet found out how to be successful in this arena.

A new role for IT

The new role for IT is nothing short of creating a revolution, the revolution of the New Organization. Its problem is (and it is not only a problem for IT) that it does not really know how to do it.

John Spackman was, until recently, the director responsible for internal computing and information services of a major division of British Telecom and has enormous experience of computerization in very large organizations and thinks likewise. He puts this new mind set quite clearly,

> ... I have for some time questioned why IT so rarely delivers the promise implicit in the capabilities of the technology. I am now convinced that we must reject the existing paradigms for investment appraisal, specification development and operation of computing systems. A new paradigm is needed where systems are based on stable corporate infrastructures to allow affordable decentralisation, where application is decentralised, but facilities are shared; where systems are

designed more for communication than for automation of self-contained processes; where systems are built expressly to assist the process of change and not to
automate current practice. The 'new organization' needs new thinking about its
information systems if it is to operate effectively in today's highly competitive
environment.[15]

Managing interdependence

In other words, Diane Wilson's transformation agenda must now come to the
fore. Her colleagues in the MIT Sloan School of Management, John Rockart and
James Short, in a major review of the different theories about the organizational
impacts of IT, find that no single approach has been satisfactory. They propose a
new agenda for IT, seeing its major role as 'managing organizational interdependence'. They recognize how organizations with sophisticated communications
technologies that help manage interdependence will, simultaneously, be increasing
the role complexity of managers. This will make life significantly harder, because
it will accelerate the necessity for team working, will require different processes
and mechanisms for measurement and will require a sophisticated understanding
of how to plan and implement changes. For many IT people who obtain their
sense of identity from their technological skills, straying into these unfamiliar
areas will, of itself, be difficult and, for some, impossible. Change they must,
however, if they are to survive.

What changes will this require? First, it will require new skills. Many more
people in IT will need to be more business aware, people aware and change
management aware. They will need to become much closer to people at the
operational end in order to understand what their expectations and hopes are of
the technology. They will need to become team players, contributing with many
other specialists to business process redesign. They will have to stop thinking of
themselves as 'IT people' and, instead, as organization developers.

At senior level, the role of IT people will change much more to one of
educating people (for example on boards of directors) to understand the potential
of the technology and to know realistically what it can do currently and what is
involved in implementing it. This will require a new breed who can provide
visionary leadership. They will have to be able to be honest about where they can
deliver the results that are needed by the business, as well as where there are large
areas of uncertainty, both in terms of the future developments in technology and
the chances of successful implementation. Much of their effort will need to be
orientated towards helping managers make informed, better-quality decisions
about IT strategies and investments.

This will involve them in much more of a 'consultancy' than an 'expert
specialist' role. Much of their work will be in trying to build some kind of shared
picture or consensus among a number of different and competing vested interests
within the organization, steering people through the minefields and sandbanks of
communications technology decisions. Their role will not be to tell people what

they *want* but help them to decide and, build commitment to, what they *need*. Above all, they will need to be very careful about managing people's expectations. This will require of them a more objective and measured evaluation of their own science and its state of development as well as a more sensitive evaluation of the organizational, political, commercial and people implications of implementing new business processes. Without such changes of mind set and skills I fear that the backlash against IT that exists in places will continue.[16] To put it more positively, those organizations that develop this kind of capability within both their senior managers and their IT people will, deservedly, gain the prize of the New Organization in terms of competitive edge, responsiveness, flexibility and the many other benefits that the New Organization seeks to bring about.

Above all, however, the new IT role will have to get to grips with the people and organizational impact of their technologies. Lutz Reuter of Digital, who has many years' experience in this field, within Digital and with its external clients, points out,

> one thing can be said right away: if IT management has an exclusive focus on the technical side of the question, the chance of rejection by the organization is very high. All the desired productivity improvements are small ... it can safely be assumed that the organizational effects will only become more visible with the ever increasing computing power ... when the technology is put in place in isolation it frequently fails. It must be put in place within a broader organization development process which integrates considerations of business direction, organization and work design, individual skills and informal social processes.[17]

Effective implementation

There are some consistent success factors that emerge time and time again from organizations' successes and disasters with IT. If more organizations paid attention to these clear lessons and steps involved in implementation, we would have more IT success stories.

Iterative scoping

The first key thing to understand is that any system has to meet the success criteria of multiple clients or stakeholders. They will not necessarily know clearly or be able to articulate *what* it is they want. Clarifying needs through an iterative process in discussions with the different stakeholders and IT people about what might be possible, is, therefore, vital. Never take a client's initial definition of need or specification at face value. The scope will always need to evolve and be developed further to gain both clarity and consensus.

Tough honesty

During this process of iteration, the IT people should be very careful that they do not create inflated expectations of what their technology can do. Equally, they should not accede to client's expectations where they feel these are unrealistic. One of the new key skills IT people may well need is the ability to say 'No'. Equally, I have frequently seen situations where one or more parties can see real impediments or blockages to the successful implementation of a system but where the bandwagon that has evolved is so strong that it is difficult to be seen as anything other than the voice of doom if you dissent. This form of individual or collective denial of problems is a major cause of project failure. Senior management in particular should ensure that IT project teams and their clients have done some kind of systematic brainstorming of all the difficulties (technical, human, organizational and financial) that might be faced and ensure that the conflicts underlying any solutions have been well worked through before taking things any further. Such constructive management of conflict leads to considerably better results. The denial and suppression of conflict or, alternatively, the imposition of a solution by one strong party on other parties is very unlikely to succeed.

Why do we want it?

A third element of success is ensuring that all parties are distinguishing clearly between inputs, outputs and impacts. The impact is the ultimate business rationale as to why the particular system is required. The simple question 'Why do we want this?' should *always* be the starting point for analysis.

The definition of outputs (in other words what the system will actually look like when constructed) must flow from the range of impacts required. Many people beyond the IT department should be engaged in the debate about the range of impacts the system is trying to achieve as well as the different options for outputs that might be available in order to achieve them. Only in informed debate can the inevitable compromises and trade-offs be made and the danger of overspecification, overfunctionality and overengineering be avoided.

Involvement

Involvement is a crucial aspect of successful implementation, but, most important is that the ultimate users be involved in the design of the system. Such involvement requires that the specialist really learns how to listen, in order that the nuances of what people are trying to express are picked up as well as hesitations or lack of eye contact, which might mean that there is still misunderstanding or unhappiness about what has been produced. Without such sensitivity, systems will never fully satisfy those who have to use them.

Regular reviewing

Finally, ensure that the project is regularly reviewed—not only by the technical team involved but by the client and user teams. These reviews are partly to ensure that the project continues to remain on target and within budgetary and time limits, but they also perform an important feedback and learning function. They ensure that what is being learnt along the way is fed back into the design and implementation process. Such regular review cycles become a very powerful mechanism for managing the inevitable uncertainties of such a project. Continuing the learning process when the system is operational can quickly result in useful, simple guidelines, such as those given in Box 8.2, that will enable users to get the best out of the system.

Box 8.2   Tips for successful computer conferencing

1   Introduce computer conferencing in a way that is appropriate to your corporate culture.
2   Select a task that fulfils a real business need. Be prepared to act opportunistically and creatively.
3   Choose topics the characteristics of which are most suited to the electronic environment—those that:

- need diversity of inputs, such as problem solving
- are important but not urgent
- would otherwise be suited to a series of meetings.

4   Provide something to motivate individuals to participate – it must be relevant to *their* work or *personal* interest.
5   Identify a suitable core group—inform them by other means about the existence of the conference.
6   Provide suitable initial training and make sure that some simple 'getting started' documentation and helpful user support is readily available in the early days.
7   Define clearly the nature and scope of the conference, for example, whether it is open or closed; what need it fills; what it covers and does not cover (refer to related conferences); the rules and guidelines for participation.
8   Invite members to enter their background, mailing details and expectations in a 'Who's Who' note.
9   Have an active organizer and good moderator to:

- throw in some topics to get things moving
- have a sense of time, asking 'Do we need to reach closure soon?' when appropriate
- keep the group focused
- pass requests on to others, create links with others
- show the links between topics
- encourage and provoke interaction
- put in some structure, such as keywords
- work behind the scenes.

> 10 Start small and grow. 'Suck and see' what works for you. Experiment and pilot. Do not overmanage—let it develop and diffuse naturally.
>
> Above all be:
>
> • practical
> • patient
> • philosophical.
>
> David Skyrme, Digital[18]

With some of these basic approaches, disciplines and attitudes in place, and as the technology itself develops, becoming increasingly able to do more what organizations require of it, we can look forward to an increasingly high success rate. Thus more of the potential of the technology can be realized. Every organization should avidly be trying to learn from others, they should be swapping their experiences and trying to discover best practice as it emerges rapidly in this very exciting but fraught field.

References

1 Jarillo, J Carlos and Howard H Stevenson (1991) 'Cooperative Strategies—the payoffs and the pitfalls', *Long Range Planning*, Vol. 24, No. 1, pp 64–70.
2 Shamoon, Stella (1989) 'From Fabrics to Finance', *The Banker*, February, pp 20–26.
3 Heskett, James L and Sergio Signorelli (1985) 'How Benetton has Streamlined', *International Management*, May, pp 79–82.
4 Grindley, Kit (1991) *Managing IT at Board Level*, Pitman/Price Waterhouse, London.
5 Rockart, John and James Short (1989) 'IT in the 1990s: managing organizational interdependence', *Sloan Management Review*, 7, Winter.
6 Stamper, Bonney (1991) 'The Competitive Market-place of the 90s: a perfect setting for EDI', *Industrial Engineering*, October, pp 25–28.
7 Stamper, Bonney (1991) ibid.
8 van Delzen, Roeland (1992) 'Learn Strategies to Prevent Runaway EDP Projects', presentation at International Project Management Conference, Florence, June.
9 *PC Plus* (1991) December, p 185.
10 Wilson, Diane (1988) 'Assessing IT Performance: what the experts say', Paper 90s: 88-050, *Sloan School of Management*, Massachusetts Institute of Technology.
11 Kamman, Alan *Global Networks, Stage by Stage*, Nolan Norton & Co., Lexington, Massachusetts.
12 Wilson, Diane (1988) ibid.
13 Corbin, Darrell (1990) 'Tying it all together: E-mail at Boeing Aerospace', *Journal of Systems Management*, October, pp 11–16.
14 Grindley, Kit (1991) ibid.
15 Spackman, John, ETIS Brussels, personal letter.
16 This was the strong feeling of senior IT people at two private research forums I spoke at in London during 1992.
17 Reuter, Lutz (1991) 'Management: the power to process shift paper', Digital, Geneva, Switzerland.
18 Skyrme, David (1989) 'The Evolution of a Knowledge Network', Digital, Reading, UK.

Pictures in the mind

Galaxies

Another image that appeals is the galaxy. Here is a huge collection of stars and other heavenly bodies in a constant state of motion that seem chaotic when viewed from outside, but, nevertheless, as great scientists have discovered over the years, possess an inherent order.

The almost magical concept of gravity, an immensely powerful but invisible force, holds all of this apparently chaotic motion together and prevents it from actually degenerating into chaos. Having said that there is sufficient energy within the system for unusual happenings. Stars come and go. Light and radiation shines from every body, every planet to every other planet, making this a good symbol of open communication. Stars shine in their own right within the galaxy—symbols of individualism and talent—but all of them cluster into groups or attract others into their gravitational field.

Part III
The software of the
New Organization

9
Holding it all together—how to stop it falling apart

The network tends not to recognize authority. If I send a paper memo I sign it 'J. Michael Watson, Managing Director'. If it is on electronic mail, then that would look ridiculous: it has to be plain 'Mike'. The new authority must come from the guidance and leadership given to them. It must be earned.

J Michael Watson, Managing Director, BICC Technologies[1]

In its efforts to become more adaptive, Becton Dickinson ran across a similar challenge. The company had dutifully created cross-functional teams and lectured everyone on the evils of bureaucracy. Even so, nothing seemed to change—the company still had too many middle managers who weren't willing to cede control to others. Said Jim Wessel, a vice-president: 'we had to get over the mind set that said, "I'm not in control so it must be out of control".'

Brian Dumaine, *Fortune*[2]

1   The nightmare of anarchy

For many managers, the New Organization looks like a nightmare scenario, a Dante's inferno of chaos, anarchy and disintegration. How can one possibly envisage unfettered open communication and organizational networking? What about overload? When will any work get done? Is it not naive to believe that any organization can exist without hierarchy? What about clear lines of authority, responsibility and accountability? How well founded, then, are these fears? Can organization members be trusted to act responsibly and put the interests of the organization above those of themselves? Does the predicted anarchy and subversion appear to happen in practice? Does the organization slide into an uncontrollable spin and decline?

The answer appears to be 'Yes' *and* 'No'. Yes, there is, in some sense, more 'anarchy', with individuals taking initiatives and doing things that they have not been 'told to do'. Many managers see in this kind of behaviour a form of heresy, while many others see in the same behaviour a release of individual talent and energy that they have been striving for. The detractors tend to see the removal of traditional forms of control as the complete undermining of the very substance of organization itself. The others, conversely, say, 'yes we have removed some of those pillars of the traditional organization, but what you fail to see is the other mechanisms of integration and control that we have put in their place'. It is cosy to fall into black and white thinking, thinking that something is either controlled or not controlled, but this is dangerous. Thinking in both-and terms, seeing all the ways in which traditional forms of rigid control are being removed, while also seeing the new forms of invisible integration and control being put in their place or alongside them, is difficult at first but far more successful, as illustrated in Box 9.1.

Box 9.1   Achieve control by giving it up!

> Change is, of course, constant—in spite of our frequent illusions about 'stabilizing' and 'back to normal'. The outdoorsman might describe it as 'permanent white water'. Don't count on things settling down in your 'business system'. Learn how to ride the rapids.
>
> The white water of our business life needs to be accepted as an endless and often uncomfortable learning curve. Consultant Bill Hunter of Cherry Hill, New Jersey, suggests that metaphors help describe today's business environment. They can also identify the secrets for management success. For example, one of the hardest lessons for a new downhill skier is to lean forward and put his weight on the downhill ski. A new skier instinctively hugs the hill. But by leaning into danger he can actually gain control. In business management today, you get control by giving it up! Like a poor skier, a poor manager works too hard on the wrong issues. New skiers who try to 'muscle in' on the slopes, trying to control the skis by sheer force instead of shifting their weight, soon find out that they are working too hard on the wrong technique.
>
> It's another way of saying that you have to leave your comfort zone and step out into the unknown. In your comfort zone you don't learn. Learning occurs in the 'danger zone'. When you search for your lost keys, don't look too long and too hard under the lamp post—to find them you will have to search in the dark!
>
> *The Foresight Intrapreneur*[3]

A different mind set is required, a mind set that can encompass the paradox that there is both hierarchy and non-hierarchy, that there is both control and non-control, that there is both participative decision making and strong direction and that there is both strong accountability and loose accountability.

Many creative idealists have perhaps seen organizational networking as the end of hierarchy as we know it. This is fantasy. It is much more helpful to think of networks as interweaving a much flattened hierarchy. It is helpful to think of strong but fewer external controls replaced by an in-built principle of self-control, self-organization and self-responsibility. It is also helpful to perceive the New

Organization as requiring multiple forms of integration to counteract the centripetal forces that may cause it to disintegrate. The stability of a dynamic object derives from the strong opposite pulls of centripetal and centrifugal forces. The same goes for the counteracting forces in the movements of the heavenly bodies and galaxies that keep the whole complicated system in a constantly changing but nevertheless dynamic balance. It is these kinds of pictures that are helpful in thinking about how we counterbalance the disintegrative tendencies of the New Organization. The New Organization may well be like the latest generation of 'fly by wire' aircraft. They have no hands-on mechanical control systems; they are flown and kept stable by software. Without it they cannot even start their engines, let alone take off.

2   Visible integration

The new networking roles

If we are letting go of some of the hierarchical and functional roles that provide the underlying structure of traditional organizations, how are we to describe what people do within the New Organization and what characteristics and strengths they need to bring to it. As the researching and writing of this book has progressed, I have become aware of a surprisingly wide range of different 'roles' that have an important part to play in the realization of the New Organization (see Figure 9.1). This is simply a list. Some of the roles overlap, indeed, many people in the New Organization will carry out something of all these roles, but some will focus on one or a few more than others. By developing our understanding of the functioning of these roles and the skills required to perform them effectively, we will be able to develop a clearer picture of how to design key building blocks of the New Organization and ensure its effective functioning.

Managers of energy

A common characteristic of all these roles is that they work the energy of the New Organization. Processes that rely heavily on networking (both soft and hard) require continuous input and effective channelling of energy because unless networks absorb and release energy continuously, they fail to function and they die. Each of these roles balances a number of energy management functions in different measure. Some of them are very important in *creating* energy, while others serve more to *attract* energy towards them or *radiate* energy outwards into the network. Others in turn are important for *boosting* or *amplifying* energy like a transformer, while others, like a pump, enable it to reach places it would not otherwise reach. Finally, some are more facilitation roles, designing methods for *transferring* energy and for unblocking blockages to *release* or *develop* energy. They are all, however, both boundary busting and networking roles, simultaneously breaking down barriers and making connections.

Figure 9.1   The new networking roles. © Colin Hastings, New Organisation Consulting. (This diagram may be reproduced freely with due acknowledgement.)

Animateur

This is a French word that perfectly describes an energy creation role. The animateur is a leadership role providing the focus and the input of vision and enthusiasm that causes others to follow. It is a more strategic role, taking the helicopter view, orchestrating and giving direction to the activities of quite a wide spectrum of people, locations and functions.

We can see it in the role of the theme leaders in the BP HSE team. Their role was to animate the activities and learning of people with a contribution to make to particular environmental issues wherever they were in the world. The Business Area leaders in ABB are animateurs of a broad portfolio of related activities throughout the world as is the role of the European region of the WHO, which acts as animateur to the total project and to all the 35 cities in this part of the project and their related networks.

Integrator

This is a generic title for what we have previously called the project leader. This is more of an operational role than that of the animateur, more focused on the achievement of tasks and the coordination of the activities of people in order to reach objectives. This is a pivotal role in the New Organization as it carries primary responsibility for the delivery of the organization's outputs to internal *and* external customers. We see this role referred to as the 'entrepreneur' within Digital, the 'agent' within DPE and the 'project leader' within the Healthy Cities Project and the Danish biotechnology industry and the 'job leader' within the BP HSE team.

Mentor

I have referred to the important mentoring role of the 'coach' at Digital and the 'sponsor' at Gore. This role is to reinforce the culture of organizational network-ing, to tune people (and particularly new ones) to the skills for operating effectively within such a culture, and to act as a sensor for problems that prevent people operating effectively. Similar roles are performed, for example, by the regional hubs of DPE, who are responsible for introducing new agents, and by the representatives at Benetton, who are responsible for finding new franchisees and inculcating them in the Benetton way of doing things.

Broker

Brokers put people in touch with each other. They do this by having very highly developed networks of their own. They gain a lot of their satisfaction from putting together different members of their network who may not otherwise come across each other. These roles are also commonly referred to as gatekeepers. Jim Bown, a senior manager in BP Research, told me that in his experience, gatekeepers are usually there to *close* doors rather than *open* them. He prefers to use the term 'window openers' instead for this reason.

Kevin Barham, of Ashridge Management Research Group, summarizes their skills well: 'they like to talk, interact with other people, show off their own ideas, hear about new ideas and explore new fields. They can form important bridges across organizational boundaries and directly or indirectly stimulate the flow of ideas, information and pieces of technology to their units'.[4] Michael Watson, the Managing Director of BICC Technologies,[5] a UK company that sells electronic networking systems, also writes interestingly about this important role,

> one fascinating fact is that when you examine the communication clusters within an organization's web of networks, you see key figures cropping up time and again. They are what are called gatekeepers: providers of knowledge to others, those people to whom everyone seems to turn for valuable nuggets of informa-tion. They can be librarians or just mavericks who are notoriously difficult to manage and who seem to produce nothing. Difficult to manage, hard to prove as profit producers and so a manager's nightmare. If we were cost cutting they might appear redundant, but take them away and the network starts to collapse.

Disseminator

These are roles that act as natural focal points for the assembly and widespread passing around of information. With E-mail, everyone becomes a disseminator but many are not practised in thinking who wants to know. Particularly important are secretaries in this regard who are key communication nodes within networks. Their role is much undervalued and underutilized. Frequently they 'think communications' when others do not and, by virtue of their roles, their awareness of the organization as a whole and its external contacts is often high. Internal media people will also become increasingly important to this end.

Investigator

These are people who love finding things out. They have a natural curiosity, an ability for detailed research and a persistent line of enquiry that enables them to access all sorts of information. Meredith Belbin, in his book *Management Teams: Why they succeed or fail*,[6] describes them as 'Resource Investigators'.

I believe there is a growing role for these kinds of people as information counsellors or educators within the New Organization. They can teach people how and where to find things out as well as to provide a service to them as the 'supersleuths' of the New Organization.

Developer

These are the people who design and facilitate organizational and business processes. They also take part in the education and development of people's skills and the organizations' core capabilities. They design conferences, workshops and training courses. They advise on different themes, roles and other elements of organizational networking.

Counterpart

These are formal roles designed to ensure that there is communication between different organizational units or locations either within or between organizations. They fulfil important liaison functions that can be specified precisely, as well as helping to create networks of contacts between the different organizations at different levels.

Their role is particularly important in ensuring the success of joint ventures and strategic alliances, but the principle can be extended into project teams and intraorganizational networks or themes where more explicit liaison between specific units is required over and beyond that provided by the informal linkages.

The multiplier effect

It may well be that a relatively small percentage of people operating key networking roles can be the pump primers who set in motion subsequent waves of organizational networking. It is instructive to think that ABB believes that it can create an organizational networking infrastructure with 500 key managers out of 214 000 employees. This is approximately 2.5 per cent of the total. While we cannot call this the 2.5 per cent rule, it does seem a reasonable hypothesis at this stage to suggest that those primarily involved in intense organizational networking can form quite a small percentage of the total organization. The multiplier effect resulting from such roles being adopted is enormous because their tentacles reach far and deep within a flattened but relatively traditional hierarchy and they move about it fluently. Equally, a relatively small group of people might network very widely both internally and externally with local, regional and global contacts. A larger group may focus their networking either internally *or* externally and, perhaps, only at a local or regional level. Yet larger numbers may network internally but within much more focused theme- or job-related areas.

3   Invisible integration

Organizational networking

In Chapters 4–8 the large number of integration mechanisms available as tools to a senior management group intent on achieving a new dynamic balance between independence and interdependence, autonomy and control in the New Organization were discussed.

We saw, for example, how each individual can become a skilful networker and teamworker. Developing their skills and networks produces powerful integrative forces. We looked, too, at the project way of working, which enables people from different functions and locations to work together, the important role of the project leader as integrator and the role of projects in focusing tasks and accountabilities. We saw how the sharing of know-how and identifying and learning from others across boundaries provides the integrative power of a common purpose. We saw the roles of hard and soft networks, the former linking the organization together with invisible electronic ties and the latter helping to bind the organization together with invisible emotional ties.

Here, already, is a potent cocktail of integrative methods, but few of them seek to control in the traditional sense of the word. They provide individuals with freedom and autonomy while also making it imperative for them to link and integrate with others in order to achieve what they as individuals wish to achieve. In so doing, they also achieve the organization's purpose. These five core elements of an organizational networking culture provide the invisible gravitational force that holds the New Organization together. There are, however, some other mechanisms, not specifically highlighted so far, that are worth summarizing. All of them are used successfully by one or more of the Pathfinders.

Senior management's role

Senior management's role in holding things together is defined by the first two parts of the book. They must provide the vision and set off on the quest, in terms of the direction in which the organization and its business is going. They discharge this role in the New Organization rather like a lighthouse or beacon. They are constantly and repeatedly talking, and reminding people, about direction and purpose, creating energy among those who find ways of identifying with that direction.

Simultaneously, senior management are managing the challenges of organizational networking. They must focus continually on the issues of collective individualism, soft networking, project working, sharing know-how and hard networks. They must concentrate their energies over a long period of time on putting in place an infrastructure that can develop these core capabilities and on removing barriers and blockages that prevent people from realizing their visions.

Transparent benchmarking

Some of the Pathfinders, for example DPE, WHO Healthy Cities Project and Benetton actually specify minimum criteria and expectations of performance for members of the network. In these cases, the criteria are related to joining the network, a process that is not common or possible for all situations. However, the practice of making their performance standards (*what* is expected of people), as well as some of the softer expectations (*how* they are expected to behave), very visible is a simple but powerful integration mechanism. ABB follows a similar principle in specifying quite precisely the performance expectations of its business areas, its countries, its operating companies and its profit centres. KWS 2000, in a very different league, specifies long-term broad performance measures for environmental improvement.

Two major principles, however, are applied to this very explicit setting of standards in the New Organization. The first is that it measures and monitors only a few key parameters of performance. As one person at Digital remarked to me, 'senior managers only measure the big numbers round here . . . they are not interested in detail'. The second principle is that of transparency. Many of the Pathfinders, though not all, make it a practice to publish throughout the network performances against the specified criteria of all major units. This is a realization in practice of a philosophy of openness, but it also provides a powerful mechanism for internal regulation as group and peer pressure, combined with a certain amount of competition, drive people to improve their performance continuously.

The new accountability

There are many who feel that processes of organizational networking fudge the issue of accountability and that you can never pin anyone down to deliver anything. Compared with the traditional hierarchical way, where people are assigned accountability, this is probably true. There are those who argue, however, that even this only provides the *illusion* of control because it still does not guarantee that people deliver. A clear new idea of accountability is emerging.

The new acountability is created by individuals and teams committing, and committing publicly, to tasks. The commitments are made not only to themselves, but to other colleagues, thus bringing in a degree of self-responsibility and peer pressure that is as powerful a mechanism as the traditional sanctions. Coupled with such a commitment approach there needs to be a cultural norm that enables people to be open when things are not going according to plan and to initiate with bosses and colleagues a process of problem solving to find ways of getting things back on track.

The New Organization culture

Organization culture, simply defined, is 'the way we do things around here'. In more formal language, it is the collection of underlying norms of behaviour, the unwritten rules that condition the *way* in which people get things done and relate to each other within the organization and those outside. It has become very clear that no amount of structural change, revised corporate strategies or new policies or systems would succeed in shifting an organization if the unwritten rules that governed people's behaviour were not also challenged, questioned and more appropriate ones put in their place.

Unfortunately, the business of creating a new culture has proved to be incredibly difficult and, in some ways, more elusive than trying to demolish the old. This is well illustrated by John Spackman, who held senior IT posts in British Telecom and now consults to Digital.

> I am intrigued by the manner in which the physical architecture of information systems reflects corporate culture and organization. BT has consistently failed to run an effective, integrated IT network despite being a vendor of networks; Digital has an extraordinarily complex and well-used internal network, although they have, in the past, concentrated on selling self-contained boxes. . . . It is very interesting to compare (them) . . . in the first case, the BT rigid hierarchy resists, in an almost organic way, any attempt towards networking; while in Digital's case the 'organism' steadfastly resists any attempt to impose more visible structures, always settling back into a networked organization.[7]

One company that has set out to transform itself radically is BP. It has invested huge amounts of money in its culture change process, which, even when there have been major setbacks for the organization, has been continuously reaffirmed. BP's aspirations to create a networking culture are summarized in Box 9.2.

9.2   Culture change in BP—a programme for action[8]

To attain our corporate vision, the management is engaged in a major cultural change programme. This is not to diminish the achievements of the past, but the market-place of the 90s is different from that of the 1970s and 80s. For instance, we need greater flexibility to respond to change. The next century will, in turn, dictate its own requirements. It will bring new demands which we must be ready to respond to.

Our culture needs to change in a number of ways. Here are some examples.

Old culture

- Hierarchies
- Boundaries
- Internal focus

Open culture

- Teams
- Connections
- External focus

- Smothering
- Second-guessing
- Controlling

- Empowerment
- Trusting
- Supportive

- Analysis
- Fear of mistakes

- Action
- Calculated risk-taking

Changing the culture means changing 'the way we do things around here' so we are evolving a new BP style.

Cultural change happens as people begin to think differently and, conse-quently, do things differently. Change applies to all of us at all levels in the corporation. Project 1990 highlighted the different kind of corporation we want. OPEN is the framework for how people should be encouraged to act in the New BP. This is not just talk—it is real, and is an active process. It begins as we act it out and is retained and reinforced as we find that it works. This is what is meant by behaviour.

When we 'walk like we talk', this is how we 'walk' in the new BP—OPENly.

Open
thinking

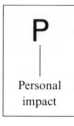

Personal
impact

Empowering

Networking

> **Open thinking** is being braver in our thinking

● **What it is**

In BP we have always stressed the importance of clear, analytical thinking. But in open thinking, we are asking people to go beyond traditional logic and technical analysis; in fact, to be braver in our thinking and to look for new possibilities around us at all levels. People who think more openly, approach problems in a fresh way—are prepared to challenge and modify the way things are currently done. They are open to considering a wide range of alternatives and are prepared to make changes in order to achieve superior results. They tend to look outwards more than they look inwards. As we all open our thinking in this way, BP will be better able to identify and respond to changes and trends in the business environment.

● **What results do we get from open thinking?**

· Openness to the ideas of others.
· Creative problem solving.
· A willingness to challenge traditional ways of doing things.
· A shift to strategic as well as tactical thinking.
· Global thinking and practices, while retaining the benefits of local variations.

> **Personal impact** is influencing others through personal example and recognition of their needs and aspirations

● **What it is**

Personal impact is the ability to influence the actions and attitudes of others through personal example and through better recognition of their needs and aspirations.

In the new BP, with fewer layers of management, influence will increasingly come from personal credibility, self-confidence and the ability to relate to and understand the position of others.

● **What results do we get from personal impact?**

· Increased awareness that any individual can make a contribution.
· Working relationships built on understanding, trust and support.

> **Empowering** is improving skills, capabilities and commitment at all levels

● **What it is**

Empowering is about improving the skills and capabilities of everyone at all levels, now and for the future. If we can all be empowered, organizational cooperation, commitment and enthusiasm will be enhanced. In the new BP culture, much more work and decision making will be delegated. To make this work, employees will need to be empowered to act and to apply their skills, and leaders and supervisors will need to develop direction, self-measurement tools and a supportive environment.

- **What results do we get from empowering?**
- Improved personal, team and organizational effort through commitment and mutual support.
- Greater flexibility in the face of business challenges.
- Individual and team support.
- Clarity of accountabilities and expectations.
- Focused energy for implementing vision and values.

> **Networking** is sharing information to achieve an objective

- **What it is**

People network naturally, but those who are going to be successful in the future will know how to network throughout the corporation. Networking is about sharing information as a positive aid to accomplishing a task or achieving an objective. Networking is simply making and using connections with others when that will help to get things done or done better.

- **What results do we get from networking?**
- Commitment to and ownership of goals and objectives by using clear, effective and sensitive communication.
- Improved and faster decision making by using effective teamwork.
- A greater understanding of the value of the interdependence of other teams and work groups.

Demolishing old buttresses

If the shadow of hierarchy is long, so is the strength of the buttresses that support it. In paying attention to culture, the senior management should not only be focusing on what new elements are required, but also on demolishing the old. When Bob Horton, the previous Chairman of BP, launched the BP culture change process, he demolished, with the stroke of a pen, a huge list of central committees that had held power for years within BP and had slowed down decision making. Roger Sant, the CEO of AES, the American builder and operator of generation plants, became aware of some of the obstacles to open communication within his organization.

At one point, workers in the plant told him they couldn't do something because 'they' didn't want them to do it. 'Who's they?', asked Sant. 'You know, "they",' replied the workers. Sant quickly realized there was no 'they', just old, inefficient work habits and memories of being throttled by bureaucracy. In response, Sant started a 'Theybusters' campaign, with appropriate buttons and posters. The result was some surprising employee initiatives. [9]

Other obvious symbols include dining arrangements, company cars, the layout and allocation of space in offices and the nature of deference and ritual in relationships between 'more senior' and 'less senior' employees. Less obvious symbols appear, for example, in the nature of contracts between organizations and their suppliers or customers. The legal department of one of my clients, which espoused the development of partnerships with its suppliers, sent me a 10-page standardized suppliers' contract for 5 days of consultancy time. I found this contract somewhat hostile. It clearly assumed I could not be trusted and placed a large number of obligations on me without placing any obligations on the company. We used this example, among others, subsequently in our culture change workshops in the company to illustrate the importance of the symbols and signals that the organization conveys to people outside the company and how these match up to its expressed intentions.

Simultaneously, however, senior management need to pay attention to how they and others can nurture an emerging new culture. My colleague, Julia Pokora, has pointed out how the sustaining of a networking-type culture is quite a different process to that of sustaining a hierarchical culture. Because the hierarchy is structured around roles, not individuals, it is sustained even when people move on as the roles and their associated systems and processes continue to exist. The networking culture, however, is nurtured by the relationships between individuals. When they move on they take these relationships and networks with them, which is beneficial in the new situation, but is difficult for those coming in to replace them. We have seen how companies such as Gore and Digital overcome this by means of their active sponsor or coach roles. Their responsibility is to help new entrants into the system to find their feet very quickly. In this manner, the culture is continuously reaffirmed and enforced where it may be in danger of dilution or gradual decline.

Moving towards and sustaining the New Organization culture does require of everyone—senior management in particular—considerable and sustained inputs of energy. New Organizations, unlike bureaucracies, are not run on autopilot nor by the rule book nor just by monitoring the numbers. It is not for those who want a quiet life. If, however, you want to stretch yourself by taking up the challenge of creating a successful twenty-first century organization, take your first steps on the New Organization journey now. I wish you good luck.

References

1 Watson, J Michael (1990) 'The Networked Organization', *RSA Journal*, June, pp 480–490.
2 Dumaine, Brian (1991) 'The Bureaucracy Busters', *Fortune*, June 17, pp 36–50.
3 *The Foresight Intrapreneur*, Newsletter by the ForeSight Group, No. 1, 1992, Goteborg, Sweden.
4 Barham, Kevin (1991) 'Networking—the corporate way round international discord', *Multinational Business*, No. 4.
5 Watson, J Michael (1990) ibid.
6 Belbin, Meredith (1991), *Managment Teams: why they succeed or fail*, Heinemann, London.
7 Spackman, John (1991) ETIS, Brussels, personal letter.
8 Extracts from BP's internal culture change booklet, 'Open up BP . . . introducing the essential behaviour', produced by BP's Corporate Communications Services, London.
9 Dumaine, Brian (1991) ibid.

Index